WAGGING TAILS *in* HEAVEN

Wagging Tails in Heaven

in

*The Gift of Our Pets'
Everlasting Love*

GARY KURZ

CITADEL PRESS
Kensington Publishing Corp.
www.kensingtonbooks.com

CITADEL PRESS BOOKS are published by

Kensington Publishing Corp.
119 West 40th Street
New York, NY 10018

All Kensington titles, imprints, and distributed lines are available at special quantity discounts for bulk purchases for sales promotions, premiums, fund-raising, educational, or institutional use. Special book excerpts or customized printings can also be created to fit specific needs. For details, write or phone the office of the Kensington special sales manager: Kensington Publishing Corp., 119 West 40th Street, New York, NY 10018, attn: Special Sales Department; phone: 1-800-221-2647.

First Citadel printing: June 2011

10   9   8

Printed in the United States of America

CIP data is available.

ISBN-13: 978-0-8065-3447-3
ISBN-10: 0-8065-3447-8

Contents

WAGGING TAILS
in HEAVEN

INTRODUCTION

Men and women are presumptuous creatures. We view the world through our unique and individual perspective and imagine that our view should be the matrix by which everyone else lives and operates. Without exception, each of us believes that if everyone were as we were, the world would be a much better place to live.

Moreover, from a collective perspective, humankind views itself as being special in this universe, and special to God, even to the exclusion all of his other creatures. Of course we're special; I don't argue that. We alone are made in his image. Not only do we physically resemble his appearance, but we are triune beings as he is a triune God (i.e., body, soul, and spirit).

Still, we ought to make room for the notion that God loves his other creatures without feeling that we are infringing on our own special status with him. I find it so unsettling to hear someone say, "Animals are for this earth only, they have no soul" or "When an animal dies, that's it for them." That is our presumptuous nature at work again.

1

Especially egregious is hearing those words spoken by those in the ministry because they are supposedly speaking with spiritual authority. They are supposed to know what the Bible says about such things and, therefore, what God thinks. The truth is that they obviously do not. As I have pointed out in many of my books (and will briefly allude to later in the text), animals do have souls, and they are important to their creator. In fact, the Bible tells us that God finds great pleasure in his animals. They please him.

He created them. He is their unseen husbandman. He feeds them, ensuring that they have sustenance. He clothes them with feathers or fur. He tells them when to migrate south or north. They are his, the creation of his hands, and he is responsible for their care. And responsibility alone is not what motivates God for the care of his creatures; he indeed possesses great love for them as well.

For man presumptuously to declare that the immutable God could suddenly change his mind and take an opposing position; that he could or would stop loving them, is simply folly. God never changes his mind. He never changes his plans. He is God. He is immutable and does not change. Change only occurs to better something, and God and all that he does cannot be bettered.

That animals have souls (or rather that they are souls), is a fact made clear in scripture. As souls, they have status with the one who created them. Biblical evidence for this conclusion has been provided in the highly acclaimed prequel to this work, *Cold Noses at the Pearly Gates*, but for the benefit of new readers, we will revisit some of the reasons we arrived at that conclusion here, but we will not dwell long on the topic.

One of the most basic truths established in the just-mentioned title is the unimpeachable fact that animals, along with all other of God's creatures (man, angels, etc.) are eternal. No exception is recorded in scripture contrary to this rule. All of God's personality-possessing creatures live forever. There is a beginning and end to physical life for animal and human, but not so to spiritual life. That life or essence is eternal, irrespective of where it is spent.

Necessarily, when we discuss the souls of animals, we cannot (nor should we try to) avoid the recent surge of alleged paranormal experiences people around the world claim to be having regarding their departed pets. People everywhere, from every walk of life, are reporting that they are being visited or contacted by their beloved pets that have passed on. It is a most bizarre phenomenon and some accounts are more bizarre than others.

Now I readily admit that strange goings on are happening in our world;:things that are unexplainable and seemingly beyond reason. From claims of Bigfoot and Mothman to UFOs and parallel universes, no shortage of mysterious topics exist. Often, the accounts of such occurrences are explainable. They turn out to be either exaggerated, or sensationalized or fabricated. But sometimes, perhaps more often than we care to admit, there are no explanations.

I accept that there are genuine unexplainable spiritual experiences as well. We live in a physical world, but spiritual or supernatural forces surround us. These forces or spirits are of both the good and bad variety. It is up to us. The Bible says to "try the spirits whether they be of God" because they are often active in our lives or the lives of those around us, and we need to know if they are of good or evil intent.

Unfortunately, accurate discernment is often hampered by the many instances of exaggerated experiences. Many desire to sensationalize or exploit a thing to draw attention to themselves or their cause. You only need to look to cable television and the host of programs dedicated to supernatural themes to know that there is a market for this genre, so the more bizarre and the more unbelievable the better. Often truth and reality are forfeited for ratings.

The radio waves are not exempt from this influence either. There are local and syndicated programs airing, predominantly in the late night and early morning hours, addressing myriad supernatural phenomenon, real and imagined. These programs draw the proverbial "nut" callers, and the bar for expert discussion is not set very high. No topic escapes being exploited, from parallel universes to shadow people who invade our homes while we sleep.

Is it any wonder then that even the topic of the souls of animals is not safe from exploitation? A smorgasbord of ideas and angles is offered for public consumption regarding the souls of animals, some good and some bad. Some are very misleading and even harmful to those who are in need of more useful and dependable guidance.

When I first published *Cold Noses* in 1996, only a couple of books narrowly fit into the pet loss genre. Today scores of titles are available, offering a wide spectrum of ideas about the souls of animals and a host of associated concerns (whether departed animals become angels, whether an animal will remember and know their people in the next life, etc.).

Any view that seems to be proven palatable to the potential reader is available and is exploited. Some of the topics covered are wild, even careless. Now if you are looking to be entertained, this will probably not be a problem for you, but if you truly want to know the answers to your serious questions, these baseless and unsupportable ideas pose a real danger to you. On matters of spiritual importance, one needs to know that what he or she is being told is trustworthy and true.

I am not condemning all the books of this genre, because some are acceptable and even a few are good. I know several of the authors personally and respect their works. I know them to be honest and eager to help. I even recommend the titles of some.

But many of the books that are available, perhaps even most of them, are baseless works, written to tickle the ears of potential readers with what the authors perceive readers want to hear. These are shameful presentations—nothing more than exploitation of those who are in pain, giving false hope and false guidance.

Sadly, those who write to profit themselves rather than to help others are not likely to know any bounds to their deceit. They will write whatever comes to mind so long as they find a market for it, with virtually no concern for whom it might hurt. Consequently, a lot of rubbish is available to people who have deep and sincere needs to be comforted. They may indeed feel comforted from the bunk they read, but like the person who hides in a closet during a fire, it is a false sense of security. In these cases much of what is written has no authority and is not true.

Scripture is the benchmark and quality-control mechanism for things discussed in this book. Some may balk at that. I cannot help the way they feel. I only know that it is the only reliable standard when discussing anything of importance. And let me turn the tables on those who would question that standard. Where else would one turn to with confidence to discern spiritual things? For me, the Bible is not just one of many resources I refer to, but the absolute rule and final authority on all the conclusions I have drawn. When it comes to things supernatural or eternal, I want guidance from the one who declares himself eternal, so I turn to the book he wrote.

Readers may therefore rest assured that the topics that follow have been thoroughly researched and held to the standard of quality control just mentioned before ever a word was written for the public. If I speculate, I will clearly identify the idea as speculation. Otherwise, you may trust that the thought, idea, or teaching is from a book much greater than the one you now hold in your hands.

Chapter 1

THE ANIMAL-HUMAN
RELATIONSHIP

B revity will be one of my main objectives for this chapter. Shelves are already filled with books on the history of dogs, cats, horses, and domesticated animals of all sorts eligible for the title of "pet." I doubt that I could add anything significant to those works in just one short chapter. Instead, I simply want to give a quick overview of the history of animals from a biblical perspective, a point of view that is seldom addressed in other books.

Predictably, I take a creationism position, but I do not do so blindly. I have studied both evolution theory and creationism and have drawn my own conclusions based on all the evidence. I doubt most evolutionists and few creationists can make the same claim. Both usually follow the lead of others and dismiss the opposite point of view as myth without having studied it out for themselves. I will not discuss the differences between these two beliefs in detail here as I address them in great detail in *Cold Noses*, and I do not wish to be redundant.

That said, the Bible tells us that originally all animals were made to companion humankind. God even allowed Adam to name them at his pleasure. I think most of us wonder where he came up with names like aardvark and platypus, but let us not concern ourselves with that here. Animal history begins with its creation. Animal history with humankind began one day later when man was created.

When the fall of humankind occurred, animals had nothing to do with it. They suffered under the curse that was brought upon this world by man's blunder. Whether that was fair or not is not in question. It is factual. Whatever history we humans have had, animals were compelled to go along for the ride.

As a result of the curse, many of the animals turned wild. Perhaps it was not so much that they became wild, but rather that God put a fear of man into them, which more closely represents the wording in scripture. That fear exists to this day. It is even present in some domesticated animals, though they are more readily befriended than their wild counterparts.

Through the ages that fear has caused a deep schism between man and wild beast. One day that will be remedied; the fear will be removed and animals will be restored to their original state of tameness. But that too is another story for another time. Since it is the domestic animals, in particular, pets, that are the focus of our study, let us concentrate on them. In so doing, I do not mean to suggest that the creator does not similarly providentially provide for wild animals. Indeed, he does. Rather, I merely want to adhere to the intent of this book and bring understanding and comfort to people regarding their pets.

Please suffer me one additional disclaimer: when I refer to pets, I will primarily be referring to cats and dogs as they represent the majority of animals kept as pets. I am not excluding horses, pigs, goats, ferrets, and a variety of other animals and exotics that have found their way into our homes and hearts. I merely want to keep it simple by not having to name all types of pets every time I use the word. Accordingly, do not feel that the things said here do not apply to your pet simply because it is not a dog or cat. That is not so.

Animals have companioned and worked for and with humans for the duration of our time on earth. Often they have played the role of working or service animals. From sled dogs to guide animals to farm mousers, they have performed services that we could not do ourselves. When a need arose that did not fit the abilities of a certain dog or cat, science and ingenuity stepped in to develop a new or diverse breed, specifically suited for the job. Evolution may want to claim some credit here, but these changes were affected by human intervention and nothing more. Even the most elementary effort at researching the development of a particular breed will bear this out.

The average pet does no work, yet is still a contributing member of the household. How many cats have awakened the family to a smoldering fire? Who guards your home from intruders with a threatening deep growl and bared teeth? Who greets you at the door after a hard day's work with a thumping tail or soothing purr? Who keeps guard over your children?

In most Western societies, pets are an important component of the home. Almost invariably they become our closest and most trusted friends. Nothing is superficial about their devotion. They accept us as we are. It doesn't matter to them if we haven't bathed. They don't wince if we use our sleeves to wipe our mouths. They don't care if we have smoker's breath. They just want to be near us. Who could ask for a better friend than that?

In the United States over 70 million households keep pets. That boils down to about 80 percent of our homes, apartments, and mobile home parks where pets are allowed. The pet industry has doubled in size and revenue twice in the last decade. There are radio talk shows, cable television shows, and community activities all dedicated to celebrating these wonderful personalities we call pets.

Across the United States there has been a substantial increase in no-kill shelters and rescue organizations as society becomes increasingly more aware of our debt to these wonderful, loving creatures. People are getting involved and contributing to the welfare of animals like never before. And I for one say, "It's about time." We owe them so much.

Many statues of and monuments to hero dogs and horses are found across this great land that they helped make so great. Museums, websites, magazines, e-zines, and myriad other initiatives that honor these noble friends of humankind are innumerable. Books, comic strips, poems, and songs have been dedicated to recognize collectively their importance to our culture. Again, it is about time. Special tributes are made to police and military K9s that gave their all to protect officers and soldiers. Even animals that were not heroic in a combat sense of the word are often given great honors. Take for instance the story of the passing of a dog named Shackles.

I will not give you Shackles' whole story, but rather pick it up exactly where it contributes to the point I am making. While an officer on active duty with the United States Coast Guard in

Hawaii, I received an electronic message from one of our isolated Loran Stations in the South Pacific. Actually, I received stacks of messages each day, mostly requests from our outlying units for additional logistics or personnel. But this one was different and I knew I had to take immediate action, so I called out to my chief: "Chief, this is a hot one," I said, somehow managing to say it in a quivering voice as I choked back tears. "Please stop what you are doing and get this message out to all units, top priority."

"Aye, aye, sir," came the customary nautical acknowledgment as the chief grabbed the message and hurried off in the direction of the Communications Center.

After only a few steps, however, apparently having read the first few lines of the message, Chief Petty Officer Smith (not his real name) stopped suddenly in his tracks and turned back toward me in disbelief. His mouth opened, but he didn't say anything. He didn't have to. I knew what he was thinking and solemnly nodded my head in understanding. Composing himself, he turned back around and headed again toward the Communications Center. The message would be electronically forwarded to major Coast Guard units in a matter of minutes for further dissemination to smaller units. Soon everyone would know.

I glanced again at my copy of the message. The officer in charge of a Coast Guard Loran Station was sending the sad news that Seaman Shackles had passed away during the night. Seaman Shackles wasn't really a seaman. He wasn't even a person. He was a dog, but a very special dog. He had been the cherished mascot of that Loran Station for over a decade.

Most of the 200-plus Coast Guard operational shore units that dot America's coastlines are staffed with a station dog like Shackles. This unofficial member of the crew is usually enlisted from a local shelter and made an honorary member of the crew. Breed and gender are not important. The only prerequisite for the job is an affinity to love and be loved. To this end, the station dog must be able to stand up to constant pampering and endure massive amounts of stroking and hugs.

Once on board the base, the station dog must also work like any other member of the crew, albeit at somewhat less demanding duties. He or she must patrol the compound (in search of handouts); escort emergency crews to their response boats (for a pat on the head); and enthusiastically greet those coming on watch (to conduct an olfactory once-over of their lunch bags).

The station dog, who was a crew member, is at liberty to dig holes, jump in vehicles with muddy feet, and borrow with impunity the only softball during a scheduled off-duty game. They are first in line at chow, are last to settle down for the night, and enjoy amnesty for anything chewed, buried, or soiled.

Generally, these animals are the best fed and most pampered on the planet, but they earn those privileges. They render a service that no other crew member can provide. They make a station a home, and that is important to service members stationed away from their real homes. Shackles earned his privileges. He made his station a home. He was eleven human years old when he passed, but during his short life he built a legacy that would far outlive him. Hundreds of sailors had been stationed at this isolated outpost during Shackles lifetime, and he had befriended them all.

In the days when e-mail and cell phones were nothing more than growing ideas in the minds of electronic engineers, families were not just a push of the button away. Often mail would take a month to arrive. Dogs like Shackles played a critical role as companion and friend. It was common for sailors to become lonely and homesick on this little strip of land in the middle of the ocean. Many found a piece of home in Shackles. He wanted to be everyone's friend. If you were lonely, if you needed a friend, he was your boy. He always had time for you. Without realizing the role he played, Shackles made life on the island bearable for many. One could run up the beach with this loving communal canine and forget, at least temporarily, that they missed Mom and Dad or the wife and kids. Over the years he had made an impact on thousands of lives in just this way.

All of them had come and gone, but he remained. The sailors were honored for their yearlong sacrifice of isolated duty with military decorations and great fanfare, but not Shackles. He remained an unsung hero, but he didn't mind. He enjoyed doing his part, and that was all the reward he needed. Nevertheless, when he passed, a fleet of heartbroken, grateful sailors finally sang his song as the message was forwarded from unit to unit. A shipmate had fallen and it was time to remember him for his service.

Shackles' story is representative of why we honor animals in our society. Some are heroes and some are workers, but all are devoted and loving companions to someone. They are dogs, cats, horses, parrots, and more; the list is indeed a lengthy one. So, too, is their history of walking alongside humankind.

I realize that there are those who do not care for animals. This is very difficult to grasp for those of us who have known the love of a pet. Nevertheless, we know it is true. There are people who absolutely have no use for animals other than a food source. There are even people who purposely abuse and misuse animals. I had thought to say something here to persuade those few to recon-sider the way they think and act, but it occurred to me that some-one who did not care for animals would not be reading this book, so the effort would be wasted.

For the rest of us it is a totally different story. We feel that no honor is too great and that no tribute too emphatic for these won-derful fur angels who have walked along with us through history and guarded our way. They are deserving of great respect and often great honor. As a side issue, I do not use the word "angel" loosely here as you shall see in subsequent chapters.

Again, there is so much we could say about the history of an-imals, but for the topic at hand, we must only establish the con-nection humankind and animal kind have shared in their history. It gives us a springboard for other, more important topics we will cover.

Chapter 2

DOES GOD CARE ABOUT ANIMALS?

You may have had difficulty figuring out what the theme of this book is from what was covered in the opening chapter. Simply, I intend to show that animals are significant creatures that are important to God. God is their creator no less than he is ours. From the importance that he places on them, coupled with the things he says in his words about them, there is much to learn about their present life and what the next life holds for them.

While I acknowledge that animals are subordinate to humans because God gave us dominance over them, too often people relegate them to nothing more than a food source or service animals. That simply is not the case. When God had finished creating them, he assessed then as being "very good," and that sounds pretty good to me. Man is wrong to assign them less worth than God does. In scripture we have a candid view of how God feels about animals. We might note at this time that the word animal does not actually appear in scripture. Rather, words like "beast," "kind," "cattle," and "creature" and terms like "every living thing" and "all that has breath" are used instead. These essentially mean the same thing, but we will use animal so there is no misunderstanding.

Our first introduction to animals is in the creation act in the Garden of Eden. Animals were made to be companions for man. They were not a food source and not beasts of burden or service animals. They coexisted with humankind in a pristine environment void of fear, disease, and death. I have often heard the word "tranquility" used to describe that first environment, and I think it is very appropriate.

The next significant mention of animals is when God clothed Adam and Eve after the fall. God clothed them in animal skins (Genesis 3:21). Later, their firstborn, Abel, made an offering unto the Lord of the firstlings of his flock (Genesis 4:4), and that offering was well received by God. Indeed, this practice of sacrificial offering would become a requirement for the Hebrew nation.

I will not discuss this practice in detail here as I address it at length in other titles, but I would like to offer a few thoughts for clarification purposes. The initial impression one has is that animals were insignificant to God because they were used for sacrifices. That is not so. In fact, just the opposite is true. They were (and are) quite significant. They were used for sacrificial purposes, which in itself spoke to the immense importance animals had to God. Animals were innocent creatures without sin. Sin offerings could only be realized with the offering of innocent blood. Without the innocent blood of animals, people at that time could not have realized atonement. I should say this underscores the absolutely critical importance of animals. Moreover, the sacrifices were a picture of the future sacrificial offering of God's only begotten Son, who would be offered as the innocent Lamb of God on the cross for sin. Until the Messiah came and his perfect blood was offered for sin, the innocent blood of animals had to suffice.

The next time animals came into special focus in scripture was at the great deluge or flood. God had Noah build an ark to preserve animal kind in the world. We all know the story, so I won't even hit the highlights here. Moving forward after nearly ten months afloat, the ark came to rest and God made a covenant with Noah not to flood the earth again. God made it a special point to extend that covenant to the animals, a very significant gesture. It speaks to their significance to him.

As we scan through the Old Testament, we are introduced to many social edicts and rules established by God that required humane care for animals. We also see passages that speak to God providentially caring for and finding pleasure in his animals. As we move into the New Testament, we see several other examples of God's tender heart toward animals. At the birth of the Lord Jesus, we see that animals were present in the stable where he was born. Some suppose that the magi from the east were also in attendance, but scripture clearly shows that their arrival did not occur for nearly two years. When the magi finally did arrive to behold Jesus, the Bible says that they saw the "young child in the house." He had grown to toddler size by the time of their arrival, and the family had moved out of the stable and into a home. The age of Jesus was further evidenced by Herod's edict to slay all the male children in Bethlehem from two years old and younger.

Then there are those who add the shepherds to the moment of his birth, but they also came after the fact. When the angels announced the birth of the Christ child to them, the birth had already occurred. They were told to go find the babe wrapped in swaddling clothes. So, except for Mary who obviously needed to be present and Joseph who rightfully was present, we are told about no other human beings on the scene at the birth of Christ. God apparently did not want them present. There were only animals, innocent animals.

It would have been a small thing for God to have made room in that inn for the birth of his Son if he had wanted him born there. It would have been easy to have had the magi leave earlier on their journey. Instead, he arranged for the event to take place where and when he wanted it to occur, in a stable with the animals. The innocent animals are important to their creator.

Many years later we see God's continued affinity for his animals when Jesus, during his forty days of fasting, spent his time not with his dearly beloved disciples but rather, as the Bible tells us, "among the wild beasts." It doesn't say, but perhaps they ministered to him as the ravens had the prophet back in the Old Testament account.

Finally, we see that God was going to restore the animals to their original state of tameness. There would no longer be predator or prey, but all would eat of the produce of the field. The fear they had for man, and man for them, would be no more. That God had a personal interest and good intentions toward animals is well documented throughout the Bible. God took a proactive personal interest in them. We are told that what we have falsely labeled "instinct" is actually the providence of God. He was the one who told them when to migrate north or south, and he was the one who provided sustenance and shelter for them.

It seemed from their birth to death, God cared about animals. Even in death he made special provisions for them. When an animal faced death, it seemed it did so more gracefully and pragmatically than we humans. As innocent creatures, they were not burdened with thoughts of being right with God as humans are. There was no need for reconciliation. They were safe in their creator (more on this later).

Accordingly, when an animal knows that its time has come, it does not seem to fear its passing as many humans do. It is as if they were given a special comfort at that time of need. Now I understand that the predator vs. prey mentality exists with animals and that each has a self-preservation mechanism that kicks in when there is danger. But when animals are ill or aged and their inevitable passing is drawing near, they seem to accept it much more gracefully than people. I can only attribute this to God's continuous care for his animals. He calms their innocent hearts.

It amazes me that some people can be so presumptuous as to speak for God. They declare that animals have no souls and that they are for this life only. They have decided that when an animal dies, God is no longer concerned about them. What of God's immutability? Can God change? Can God change the way he feels? Can he stop loving his creatures? Does he punish the innocent? The answers are of course no to each of these questions. If God cares about an animal, he will care forever about that animal. If this were not so and if we could not depend on God to be constant and true, how could we place trust in our relationship with him?

If he were as whimsical as some make him out to be, how precarious would our position be? Would we be at risk of God being in a bad mood on the day we passed? Would God be able to change his mind about our reconciliation with him? Thankfully, the answer is again no. We can depend on the immutability of God. Not only will he not change, but his nature will not allow for it. He is perfect and constant.

Chapter 3

DO ANIMALS HAVE SOULS
AND AN AFTERLIFE?

A t some point in our lives, we have all lost precious and dear pets or at least have knowledge of someone who has. Their passing is often as painful to us as when we lose human loved ones, sometimes even worse. When they leave us, we like to think that there is a place for them in eternity. We need to feel that somehow, someway, provisions have been made for them.

Unfortunately, when we seek validation for these hopes from those we look to in spiritual matters, we frequently find that they hold to the view that animals are for this world only and that they do not possess eternal souls. We are told that when they pass, that is the end of the road for them. Since we hold our ministers in high esteem and trust what they say as authoritative, this seemingly qualified disclosure only serves to deepen our sorrow and pain.

I know this pain firsthand, for this very thing has happened to me. I am sure my story will resonate with many who have experienced a similar situation. Mine took place at my church just before an evening service. "Why Brother Gary, what seems to be the matter? You look like you just lost your best friend," my pastor's wife said as I made my way to my usual pew. I actually had noticed her making her way toward me, but because I really did not feel like talking with anyone, I had tried to detour around her. Though a rather large woman and not very quick on her feet, she somehow managed to get ahead of me and intercepted me anyway. I didn't respond immediately because as I previously stated, I just didn't feel like socializing. I had a very heavy heart. She had pinpointed my problem exactly. I had indeed lost my best friend. My beloved dog of sixteen years had passed away the day before, and I could focus on little else but the terrible void and sense of loss I was feeling. I probably shouldn't have been out in public so soon because I surely wasn't my normal lighthearted, outgoing self. But I was feeling particularly low just before church and thought how wonderful it would be to have the support of those of like faith. That might actually help ease the pain I was feeling. So, I dragged myself out in the hope that I could find some relief from my grief in the compassion of others.

For just a brief moment it seemed my hope was about to be satisfied. The pastor's wife wore a big smile as she continued to speak, "You are always such a happy person and today you look so glum."

As I sought for something to say, I felt tears welling up in my eyes. I knew that I had to squeeze an answer out quickly or risk blubbering incoherently as my emotions took over. So I quickly blurted out, "My dog died yesterday."

Sure that she heard the quivering in my voice and saw the tears beginning to flow, I waited for the compassionate words that I knew only a pastor's wife could find. My wait was not a long one as her response came quickly. To my horror, instead of offering sympathy and compassion, she sarcastically said, "Oh, and I bet you think your dog went to doggy heaven don't you," followed by what I can only describe as a dismissive, sinister laugh.

I didn't know what to say or do. Her words stunned me. And the fact that I was stunned was itself unsettling. It was so unlike me to be caught off guard for any reason. I never jump at loud noises or when people jump out from behind a door to scare me. I never wince when someone at work lets fly expletives that would make a sailor blush. I have learned to expect people to say the unexpected and not to be caught speechless. But all that changed in less than a moment. A handful of unexpected, hurtful words distorted my reality and sent me mentally reeling. I struggled to keep my composure and to find some appropriate way to respond, but nothing would come. Sadly, and shamefully, my only recourse was to resort to the tactic most people resort to when they find themselves in an awkward situation that they do not want to deal with at that moment: I forced a stupid grin and chuckled nervously. And then I just walked away.

I didn't want to grin. I didn't want to chuckle. I didn't want to walk away. I wanted to lash out and admonish her for her callousness. I wanted to ask her if she treated all who expressed a need for encouragement with such a lack of compassion. I wanted her to know that she'd kicked me when I was down and that she was not a very good pastor's wife. But I didn't say any of those things. I didn't have it in me at the time. It just wasn't that important at the moment. I couldn't handle a confrontation. I just wanted to be left alone, and so I chuckled and walked away. Outwardly, I erased any sign of hurt or anger toward her, but inwardly I was mortified. She had taken one of the most traumatic experiences of my life and heaped more grief and pain upon it. Her undeserved cruelty to me was bad enough, but the dubious sentiment she expressed about the souls of animals was even more disturbing.

I was to find later in my research on this topic that many in ministry shared her negative and erroneous view of animals and the afterlife. I also discovered that many other people who have kept and loved pets were experiencing the same reaction from their respective ministers when they sought encouragement and understanding. I have received hundreds of letters and e-mails from exasperated churchgoers who have suffered similar calloused responses at the hands (or words) of their ministers. Sometimes it was from direct dialogue about a specific pet, but more often it was just hurtful and insensitive comments made from the pulpit that suggested animals were not important to God because they were creatures without souls.

Overwhelmingly, mainstream denominations hold to this opinion. They imagine (and I do not use this word lightly) that animals are temporal creatures without souls. The usual premise for this belief is that the Bible says that God breathed life into Adam, but does not say that he followed the same prescription to animate animals. People imagine that this means God somehow transferred his spirit to man. Hence, in their mind man has the Spirit of God in him and animals do not. I find this position both theologically immature and wholly unsupportable by scripture. That animals have souls is an unimpeachable teaching in scripture. To discover this requires the most elementary of studies, and yet many will not put forth the effort. They would rather take the word of someone else, who took the word of someone else, who—well, you get the idea.

So let us study this matter out for those who have not or will not take the time to do so. The word "soul" is used in over twenty different ways in scripture. When it comes to animals, the Hebrew word "nephesh" is used. This word translates to the words "essence" or "life." The word confers permanence to that life. It is not and cannot be assigned a temporal value when using this word. God is the one who gives this soul (nephesh) life. Whether he literally breathes that life into each soul or not is not at issue. This is a criteria concocted by man's imagination and nothing more. Animals live. They have life. That life has to come from God as he and he alone is the source of life. Adam could not do it. All life comes from God.

Moreover, if having God personally breathing into someone was the prerequisite for having a soul, because it was not recorded that God breathed life into animals does not mean it did not happen. It very well could have happened exactly that way. But again, it is a moot point as it does not matter whether he did or did not. Moot or not, let me graduate the question a couple of steps further to emphasize my point. If the prerequisite is that God must personally breathe into a person in order for them to have a soul, than what of women? We are not told that God breathed life into Eve. So Eve had no soul? And are we to assume then that not all women have souls?

If we follow the pseudotheology of this erroneous view, it

becomes even more outrageous. We must conclude that the only man who had a soul was Adam, for God apparently did not breathe into every man. Adam may have been able to pass along physical traits to his offspring, but the soul comes from God. So, if God did not breathe into each man, each man did not receive a soul. How foolish an idea is that when you follow it out to the extreme.

The idea that animals do not have souls is erroneous. There is no biblical support for such a position. Indeed, there is overwhelming evidence proving that they do have souls and are eternal creatures by virtue of having a soul. This conclusion is not hard to arrive at. An elementary study of pertinent scripture is all that is required. Anyone who wants to know this truth can find it with ease. No one should have the facts wrong on this matter, in particular those whose responsibility it is to know what scripture says. Those who call themselves ministers should necessarily be prepared to minister. They should have answers ready for others who depend on their advice, and not making the effort to study this topic out is egregious.

Many ministers need to revisit their ideas about animals and animal afterlife. Trusting what they heard from their seminary professor or a previous pastor is not acceptable. The onus is on them to know the facts for their flock. Their calling is one that puts them in a position of trust. They are in the ministry to serve and help when members of the flock have needs. Losing a beloved pet is indeed a time of great need. It is not a time when a minister wants to come up short.

It is a lazy and spiritually dangerous practice to disregard the Bible's instructions "to search out whether these things are true."

Ministers take on an obligation to have ready and sound answers for their congregants, in particular when it comes to matters of the heart. People go to church to "know" what God says, not what a seminary professor thinks. A minister must know, not hazard a guess.

If you are a minister or if you have a minister who has either expressed a negative view on animals having souls or been un-receptive to your needs in this area, you may want to share the following passage and explanation with that individual. I would recommend you do so with a kind spirit and not let it turn into a confrontation. Your goal should be to help, not hinder.

In perhaps the oldest book of the Bible, the Book of Job 12:10, it tells us, "In whose hand is the soul of every living thing." This is a very profound passage. The initial, layman, face-value per-ception is that God is speaking of all creatures, human and an-imal. It seems quite simple with no need of higher criticism. But for the sake of argument, the considered, in-depth study of the passage supports the initial perception. God is speaking of all creatures, human and animal.

As I mentioned previously, the word "soul" is used in over twenty different ways in the Bible. Invariably, when people come across this word in scripture, they automatically associate it with redemption. It happens so often that in no matter what context the word is used, the connection to reconciliation and salvation is always present in the person's mind and unconsciously applied to the interpretation. In most cases, this is right and acceptable to the rules of exegesis, but there are times when it is not. Clearly, the gospel message is not for animals. It is exclusively for peo-ple. It is a reconciliatory outreach from God to people through his Son. However, to allow this truth to cause one to draw the conclusion that an animal therefore cannot have a soul is to visit a gross injustice upon scripture.

The Hebrew word "nephesh" appears many times in scripture, and it is used interchangeably to describe both the essence of man and animals. It does not make a distinction between the two, and it does not delve into salvation in its application. Rather, it addresses the consciousness and, sometimes, the eternal characteristic of the soul.

This passage in Job is a good example of this. The word "soul" is not used in relation to redemption but rather addresses providential care and the length of time that care lasts. A clearer meaning of this verse would be, "In whose hand is the life or essence of every living thing." God is speaking of that part of humans and animals that contains or houses the life he has given to them or that part that departs the body when the body expires.

When we mesh this thought in Job with Romans 8 and Revelation 5:9–13, to name a few corresponding passages, the meaning is clear. The life or essence of every living thing is in the eternal hands or care of the one who created that life.

However, this word in Job indicates an even deeper thought for us to consider. We often refer to man (or woman) as a flesh-and-blood body with a soul. That is not so. Up to this point, I have been categorizing the soul in that way because I had other peripheral points to make and did not want to confuse readers.

Now that we have accomplished that, it is time to set the record straight on what the human soul is, and what it is not. In keeping with the absolute intent of this Hebrew word, man is a soul that has been placed in a flesh-and-blood body. Man is not a body that contains a soul; man is a soul housed in a body. The distinction is subtle, but it is immense in effect. This is our essence, that we are a soul, not a body. The body is temporal, but the soul eternal.

This truth applies to animals as well. They are not creatures with souls, but are eternal souls given temporary bodies. The same word is used to describe their essence as it is ours. So when we refer to their souls, we are merely acknowledging that animals have essence and that this essence is eternal in nature. They are like us in that way, but unlike us in that they need no salvation. They are innocent creatures with souls. Those souls are safe in the hand of their creator.

In fact, I see nowhere in scripture where any living thing God created was made to be temporal. Humans, animals, and angels are all eternal beings. Being eternal means their lives do not end. The body will expire, but the soul, its essence, lives on eternally.

It has always seemed presumptuous to me that my fellow ministers would shoot from the hip on this topic rather than expend a little energy to discover what the Bible actually teaches. How they can imagine that these precious, devoted, and loving personalities we call pets will perish forever, while on the other hand acknowledging that scripture teaches that God allows the wicked Satan and his horde of evil demons to continue to exist forever is simply outrageous.

I know that the Bible says that Satan and his demons will suffer under the wrath of God for all eternity, but it also says that they will never be completely done away with. They will in fact live forever. This may come as a shock to some, but there can be no doubt that while Satan hates God, God still loves Satan.

He hates his evil. He hates his wicked rebellion and sin. But he loves the creature he made. How presumptuous for men to think God would stop loving the innocent animals he made. Those who cannot understand this are ignorant of God's unchanging nature. God is immutable. His original plan was that man and animal would live forever. He has not changed his plan. It is still in effect. God never changes.

Before we move on to the next chapter to discuss what the afterlife will be like for animals, I wanted to briefly address a different yet associated matter that I feel best fits here. As I have shown in the preceding, it is easy to see how those we look to for spiritual guidance can cause us emotional harm through their ignorant neglect of scripture. But there are also ministers and spiritual leaders who can do us emotional harm by ignorantly adding things that are not in scripture.

Let me explain: Several years after publishing my first title, *Cold Noses,* many copycat books came on the scene. In my opinion, some are acceptable works, but many are not. To have their fifteen minutes of fame, it seems some authors would go to any lengths. Some delve into the weird and bizarre, while others seemingly claim divine revelation. Authors offer unique ideas but no proof or evidence of their claims.

An array of "insights" can be found about ghostly pet visitations (which we discuss in detail in chapter 11), pet psychics, and myriad other topics aimed at tickling the ear of the reader. Most of the authors' revolutionary ideas are outrageously unsupportable by any acceptable method of higher criticism and largely self-defeating when you really explore what they are attempting to say. These are so obviously bizarre that most readers immediately dismiss them as unsupportable opinion. But a few of the ideas are appealing to readers. They play to the heart and seem spiritual enough at face value to warrant a closer look. Then if the author's literary skills are adequately persuasive, the reader more readily accepts those ideas without the required proof, though they are nothing more than notions.

One such notion that has found fertile ground to grow in is that the pets of Christians will be part of the rapture, that well-documented, well-known Christian event in which the Son of God will whisk living and nonliving believers from the earth and take them to heaven immediately before the seven-year period known as the Great Tribulation. The idea that pets of professing Christians are to be part of this event is not only new but New Age. By that I mean the belief is based on a philosophy of "it feels right" rather than exegetical evaluation of canonical or historical evidence.

Now I love animals, and if there were any way that I could even loosely make this notion fit with scripture, I would. But that simply is not the case. Some accused me of embellishing on my research in *Cold Noses*, saying I made the scripture fit my bias. That is not so. As I explained in that book and state again here, if scripture had offered up a completely different conclusion on the souls of animals, I would have sadly reported that fact. Fortunately, it did not.

On this idea of pets being part of the rapture, I would love to be able to report that it is true, but it is not. That a pet could somehow, through osmosis, or some other process or mechanism, be a participant in this event is preposterous. That is not at all in keeping with what scripture teaches. The cornerstone passage that addresses this event is found in 1 Thessalonians 4 in the New Testament, and it is exclusionary when it comes to anyone else but believers. These verses clearly establish that human believers are the only participants of this translation. The book is addressed to the "church." That the book is addressed specifically to the church of the Thessalonians is not problematic. Though written directly to the Thessalonians, the things recorded in this and all the other books and epistles of the New Testament apply to all true believers, irrespective of their geographic location or the time they lived in history. Consequently, each believer can understand that this great translation is for him or her and no one else.

The purpose for this event is singular. Christ returns to remove his church (all believers in Christ) from the earth so that they (all believers) do not experience the great tribulation. The whole event is the bridegroom coming back to receive (and rescue) his bride, the church; and taking her (them) to the marriage supper of the Lamb. That is an oversimplification, and I hope I have not offended any of my fellow theologians, but in a nutshell, that is the primary purpose of this translation event.

There is no hint of any animal, angel, or nonbelieving human being included. The wording is not ambiguous. Indeed, it is as clear in this passage as anywhere else in scripture. The rapture is for members of the church and no one else. Another good passage that illustrates this is Matthew 22. Here we are told the story of someone who tried to invite himself to a marriage feast without the proper credentials, if you will. The king ordered that he be bound hand and foot and cast out. The rapture is a marriage feast and only those with a proper invitation (those who know the Son) are bid *come*.

The bottom line: animals are not part of the church and there-fore not part of the rapture. Admittedly, this presents a very big dilemma for people who love their pets. Necessarily, if the ani-mals do not join their believing people during the translation, the only alternative is that they will be left behind. I cannot deny that. It appears that this will be the fate of those animals that are part of Christian families when the rapture occurs. The initial, gut reaction to this revelation is one of anger and blame. If the animals are left behind, most will suffer without food or water and many will die. Why would God allow animals to suffer like that? Why would he allow such a thing? It is so cruel.

I have some common sense ideas and suggestions on how to avoid your pet suffering that I would like to share with you. But before we get into that, I think we need to set the record straight on where blame should be affixed. We are always quick to blame God, not necessarily because he caused something bad to hap-pen to us, but more likely because we feel he could have stopped it from happening, but did not. Somehow, whenever something bad befalls us, no matter that it is a direct result of something we did or did not do, God is to blame. I suppose that is just human nature.

However, the truth is if God had his way, things would be different on this earth. There would be no need for the rapture, no need for reconciliation, and no need for faith. We would still dwell with God and see and fellowship with him daily. Earth would still be the utopia he started us out with. It was human nature, not divine nature, that changed everything. It was man who caused the fall, not God. It is man who has made this world the woeful place that it is. It pays no dividend to blame God. If he had his way, life would be wonderful and perfect, as he intended for it to be. By our own hand and choice, we have what we have. If there is any blame at all, it belongs to the one who stares back at us in the mirror.

We have desired free will from God and he has given it. We do not want him interfering with our decisions, but we still want him to have our back when those decisions cause the world to turn against us. God has given us the control we all want and though it pains him to see us suffer, he restrains himself from intervening against our will. One day he will set it all straight, but for now he endures and suffers along with us for our sakes. It is unfair of us to demand we have control; we exercise that control, and then blame him when things go wrong.

Irrespective of all that, we are still faced with the dilemma of pets of Christians being left behind. It may not be this generation, or the next, or the next. But one day there will be a generation of Christians who will be snatched off this earth without warning, and their pets will be left behind to fend for themselves. For many families, there will be a family member or two who never put their faith in the Lord and they will be left behind, so it will not be a problem. For those whose whole family was composed of believers, the cold, hard truth is, the animals will still be left behind alone. There can be no doubt that some will suffer and eventually perish. Sadly, that already happens many times each day. It is a world of woe and grief. The only solace I find in this is knowing that when they pass, they awaken to a new world where that can never happen again.

There will be those instances where neighbors or other relatives will discover your absence and step in to care for the ani-

mals, but I think more often than not, it will take time to come
to that point, and for many of these fine, noble creatures, it will
be too late. For that reason, here are some steps I have taken or
recommend to ensure that our best friends have the best chance
of survival in a postrapture world:

1. Always keep enough food and water available to last at least
    thirty days. It takes a little planning and effort, but on any
    given day my three dogs have sufficient water and dry food
    available to them. I check the water levels daily and clean
    bowls weekly to maintain quality. The food is kept unopened
    in the original package to avoid odors building up or the food
    going bad. If needed, I know they will tear the package open
    themselves. Oddly, I know that they would not even con-
    sider eating this dry food if I offered it to them today. They
    would turn their noses up at it and not give it a second
    thought. But given a week's hunger, I know it would be much
    more attractive, and so I leave enough for them to last for at
    least thirty days.

    My thought is that 30 days is sufficient time for people
    from work, relatives, or neighbors to have grown concerned
    enough about my family's whereabouts to call the authori-
    ties. Assuming the authorities will enter your home, it prob-
    ably would be a wise idea to have some easy to find directions
    on what to do with your animals (who to call, any assets you
    have set aside for their care, etc.).

2. In one situation I arranged with a non-Christian neighbor
    who I was friends with to check on my animals if he had not
    seen me for a week or so. I explained my situation and

thoughts to him, and while he raised an eyebrow at my request, we were close enough that he reluctantly agreed. I think he initially felt that I had found a unique way to preach religion to him, but he soon realized that I was serious, and he respected my beliefs. If you use this method, please ensure that you let your neighbor know when you are going on an extended vacation. Otherwise, you may come home to find your front door broken down, your neighbor in jail, and your friendship a bit strained.

3, Put your pets in your will or other legal trust documents. This should ensure that once they are rescued, they are not just sent to a shelter to a situation worse than the one they were rescued from. Set aside financial assets to cover their anticipated expenses. Prearrange with a close friend or relative, who again is not a believer, to take over the care of your pets and assure them you will set aside sufficient assets to cover their living needs.

Probably other innovative steps can be taken if you think about your personal situation a bit. Still, I would not stress too much over this concern. I know it is painful to think about, but the silver lining to this dark cloud is that should your animal suffer and pass away, the result will be that they are with you again. Somehow to me that is much more attractive than my pets having to survive in the awful tribulation period.

Chapter 4

WHAT WILL THEIR AFTERLIFE
BE LIKE?

A s with some questions regarding the eternity of animals, little to nothing is mentioned about this topic in the Bible. The fact is that the Bible was written for man and not animals, so direct answers to questions are hard to come by. A less direct approach is called for. Because God is consistent in how he deals with his creation, we can indirectly apply the questions about animals to people and draw some pretty solid conclusions.

In other words, in order to understand what heaven will be like for the animals, we simply need to look at what it will be like for people. The bad news: unfortunately, not a lot is said in the Bible about what this place will be like for people either. In fact, little mention is made of this place at all until almost the end of the last book of the sixty-six books that comprise the Old and New Testaments.

Fortunately, what little is said is enough to assure us that heaven is not anything like earth. The world we now occupy is a complete aberration from what God intended it to be. This world has fallen out of fellowship with God and into immorality, injustice, suffering, sorrow, and death. Everything that comprises this world is in some state of decay or deterioration. Not so this place called heaven. The Lord tells us in Matthew 6:20 that it is a place "where neither moth nor rust doth corrupt." There is no deterioration and no decay. Indeed, we are told it is a world void of fear, pain, illness, want, anguish, sin, sorrow, or death. It is a place of life that neither wanes nor fails. It is unlike anything we can imagine because our only experience has been this life of woe and decay. Men and women can only draw from their experiences. We cannot for instance, fully appreciate or understand the infinity of God, for we ourselves are finite. When one ponders the existence of God (and we all have done this), our minds slam into the wall of our own limited experience, and we cannot grasp that God has always existed. Surely, there must have been a start for him? Where did he come from? Who made him?

Because of this, our thoughts of heaven often feel like nothing more than pipe dreams and fantasy. That such a wonderful place could exist goes against all that we have experienced and know. But our limited perception and ability to grasp infinite concepts does not change the fact that all the Bible says is true and will come to pass. Indeed, we have an afterlife, and for those who have met God on his terms and reconciled to him, this place of wonder and great appeal is a certainty. The only obstacle that prevents us from enjoying it is time, but time will fail and not prevent us.

This place is also for the innocent animals God created to enjoy. For the naysayers, I will allow that it is possible that God will have made a special place for them apart from where humans will be. In the absence of detailed guidance, that is a possibility, but not a probability. We have no reason to believe that God would change what he set in place in the relationship between humankind and animals. We were made to live side by side here and have no reason to think that formula will ever change. God changes not. Furthermore, the Bible alludes to animals being in heaven at this present time. There are the beasts around the throne that give praise to God, the horse that Christ will return on, and several other references to animals. Believing animals are welcome in this place is reasonable.

Too often people make the erroneous assumption that heaven is a place God made for people. It is not. It is a place he made for himself. We are merely invited there if we will reconcile to him on his terms. The angels are also there by God's will and invitation. It only makes sense that the third type of his creatures, the animals, will also be extended this courtesy. That does not mean that heaven will not be customized for people. God is a gracious host, and he has designed heaven to accommodate people and their needs. What little physical description we are given of this wonderful place seems to be for our benefit and comfort.

Here are just a few glimpses beyond the pearly gates. I won't bother to quote a lot of scripture as most of the physical characteristics of heaven are given in the last two chapters of the book of Revelation, and you can easily read about them if you so desire. They'd take up much-needed space here.

Briefly, we are told of the jeweled foundation and gates of the great city, of the streets made of seemingly transparent gold, of the river of crystal, and the rainbow around God's throne. This place is of great wonder and splendor, unlike anything we have

imagined in our earthly experience. The entire place is illumi-
nated, not by some wonderful new sun or star, but by the actual
glory of God—a light that casts no shadow, but illuminates unlike any light previously known. Our enjoyment of all that God
has made will be pure and holy for we have been given new, glorious bodies that are free from sin and self-centered concerns,
such as gain, greed, anguish, and sorrow.

Heaven will be the new world or existence that animals will
enjoy along with us. They will be an important component to
the eternal home because they are important to their creator. He
finds great pleasure in the life his hands created. Here they will
be as they once were: tame and companions to humankind. They
will join the angels in our worship and praise of the Lord and
us. Coincidentally, this is one of the reasons I think that they will
likely have the ability to communicate as I believe they once did
in Eden. For them there will also be no death or pain. Their new
life and experience will mirror ours.

Now then, what will the actual heavenly experience be like?
That is a whole new can of worms to open, not only because this
topic produces such a diverse array of ideas, but because this is
another topic not addressed in great detail in scripture. I suppose one reason the Lord does not give us detail is that he places
more importance on ensuring that we get there rather than on
our actually being there. So his focus in his Word is to tell us
how to get there. However, he does give us glimpses. We do
know that we will be joint heirs with Christ, and that this will
entail quite a few benefits from the Father. We also know that
we will have a wonderful mansion (some define this as a "room"),
that heaven will be a beautiful and glorious place, and, above all,

that we will be happy. Happiness can be subjective. A little girl once asked a well-known celebrity preacher if her pet would be in heaven. His response was words to the effect "If that is what it takes to make you happy in heaven, your pet will be there."

While I agree that pets and all animals are eternal creatures, I do not agree with the context in which he framed his thoughts. If indeed heaven would be whatever it took to make us happy, what would make it different from the earth? Would not a drug addict want drugs? Would not a king want to rule? Invariably, the philosophy stated by this preacher is one shared by all of us on some level. Who has not said something like "When I get to heaven there is going to be a football game on television every night" or "Heaven is going to be fishing every single day"?

Thinking this way is just human nature. If heaven is going to be a place of happiness, we have a list of things that will make us happy. The problem is that human nature is sensual. We are sinful. We are self-centered. You may deny it, but you know it is true. Even our most noble and benevolent thoughts and gestures are designed to make us feel good about ourselves. All that we do is centered on that most important person, me. We are told in 1 Corinthians 15 that we are corruptible creatures, but that "this corruption shall put on incorruption." I don't want to go into great detail here, but suffice it to say that when a Christian is translated, through either death or rapture, the old nature or corruption is left behind.

The new or divine nature of God takes control, and the things that would have made our old corruptible self happy, no longer will. Now, new things and better things will make our new nature happy. It remains to be seen what that will entail, but the result will be different and it will be appropriate to our new life and complement the holiness of God. The verdict is that heaven will be a place of unprecedented happiness just as God promised. Heaven will be happy for humans, animals, and angels, but not because it conforms to us, but because we are conformed to enjoy heaven's higher and better things. So indeed, animals will be there, but not because it will make us happy that they are. Rather, they will be there because God has said they will live forever.

Chapter 5

WILL ANIMALS LOOK LIKE THEY DID ON EARTH?

S ome have asked me, "Does it really matter what animals will look like? Is it really important? Shouldn't we be more concerned with what we humans will look like?" Questions like these seem more like indictments of my motives rather than honest inquiries. I feel some think I consider animals more important than people. I do not. What our animals look like in the next life is of interest to many people, in particular the kind of people who read books like this. Whether the topic is important in and of itself is not the point. People who love their pets want to know, and that makes the topic important. A need exists and I merely am trying to meet that need.

Humans are God's most prized and cherished creation. There can be no doubt about this. We are made in his image. Animals are not. Angels are not. That is an honor only we people enjoy. All that God has done in our reality from creating our world to filling it with life has been for us. We are his focus. We are the object of his affection and interest. All else is secondary. That does not mean that everything else is insignificant or unimportant. Animals may not be made in God's image, but he created them and they are important to him. He provides shelter and sustenance for them. He directs their seasonal migrations. When it comes to domesticated animals, he gives specific instructions concerning their care and well-being. Animals are not insignificant to their creator.

Animals are no less the work of God's hands than we humans are. Scripture tells us that he finds great pleasure in them. He created them with sovereign design, giving them diverse shapes, sizes, coatings (feathers, fur, scales, etc.), abilities, and functions. Each animal serves a purpose in its respective environment. That purpose may not be substantial, but it is undoubtedly significant and important.

Evolution theory would take what God has done and give credit to the creation rather than the creator. It would have us believe that animals somehow have the capacity to see ahead many millennia and take action to have an impact on the future of their species. Somehow, they are able to determine what will be needed by their descendants to adapt to conditions that will exist at some future date.

I don't want to get off on a rabbit trail here, but humor me for a moment while I ask a couple of provocative questions about evolution. How can any intelligent person believe that the *dumb animals* (their words, not mine) could somehow consciously possess the intelligence to perceive the future and instigate a change process to ensure that the species survives?

Do scientists truly realize that they are claiming that animals can develop new characteristics and physical features simply by initiating the process and passing the torch along for thousands and perhaps millions of years to their descendants? For example, could a fish develop a bump and then pass the torch to its offspring to develop a toe and so on for several generations until a foot somehow mystically developed in the womb of a descendant one hundred generations later?

This idea is not only presumptuous but preposterous. If animals were capable of such intelligent planning, why would it take millions or even billions of years for them to evolve to the level they desire? I mean if they have the ability to change, why wait? Humans, who supposedly have enormously greater intellectual capacity, are not able to coordinate such things, but we easily and readily ascribe to animals a higher capacity to achieve with a much lower intelligence? We humans cannot even agree on the facts of historical events that happened just a few hundred years ago, but somehow animals are able to work together with nature to orchestrate an intelligent design of evolution that bridges billions of years?

Moreover, how come a current generation could not develop some elementary or basic advances? For instance, why is it that a few generations of opossum and raccoon have not evolved enough to understand the dangers associated with asphalt or automobiles? Surely (and very sadly), their field-testing experiences have been extensive and given them enough data to make some changes.

Let's take evolution theory to one of the many extremes that naturally (pardon the pun) arise if you think the presumption through. Boil down all the natural selection ideas, and what you come up with is simply this: that nature (flora, fauna, and environment) works together somehow, coordinated by some unseen force, to decide how they will evolve. Science says that the unseen force is the combined effort of the components of nature working together, whether consciously or subconsciously. This raises some questions for me: Which of them made the key decisions? Who decided the order of things? Which of these visionary, super perceptive creatures stepped up and volunteered, and said, *"Hey, I think I'll be prey"* or *"Ooh, ooh, can I be the one with the least longevity?"*

Nature is a wonderful balance of components that seem to operate well on their own. No evidence has been found proving that the animal kingdom consciously and purposely works together to make nature a success. If that were so, deer would stand still and accept their fate rather than fleeing the cougar. But they do not. Prairie dogs would mark their many burrow entrances to warn buffalo of the footing danger. But they do not. I simply cannot accept that either a species could coordinate biological changes for their kind or the collective animal kingdom could work out their mutual differences, the intricacies of their diverse environments, and the way they overlap each other. So it is a very safe bet that I will not accept random happenstances in nature allowing for natural selection or survival of the fittest. That may be true on an individual case-by-case basis, but not specieswide.

Rather, I see design and providence in it all. Even ardent evolutionists believe that there seems to be an unseen force that oversees the order of nature. While some believe random chance brought together a million life-essential details, concentrated all on one obscure planet among perhaps 1,000,000,000,000 or more planets that have not even one of those life-supporting details, I simply cannot. The order of nature is just too complex and too perfect to be the product of chance. I find it easier and more prudent to accept that there was and is a creator. Possibly, hundreds of billions to trillions of planets and stars hang on nothing, and yet they are held in place. Our own planet consistently rotates and tilts to create life-sustaining seasons, replenishing itself where and when needed. There undoubtedly is a superior intelligence behind it all. The results are just too complicated and complex to have been the effect of a big bang and subsequent natural selection.

Turning back again to the theme of this chapter, it would seem that every animal was created to look exactly the way it looked from its start. Each has a specific role in its respective environment, and its environment supports its specific needs. I will not argue that there are no oddities in nature. Certainly there are. But because I do not understand why an animal was created the way it was does not mean it was not made exactly right for its environment and purpose.

Scientists will tell you animals are still evolving, and if we could take in the whole evolutionary picture of billions of years, we would see it more clearly. No concrete evidence of that exists. In fact, that is the cop-out safety net for evolution theory: to claim that changes occur over such a long period of time that we cannot see them actually happening.

The failsafe for this cop-out is to drag out some old bones or teeth and build a creature around them, something that has often proven to be very embarrassing to scientists in the past. Many of the claims of early evolutionists have proven not only to be flawed but also to be ridiculously false, and yet they continue to

make newer, more informed claims. Indeed, if you were to compare what evolutionists believed in Darwin's time to today, you
would find evolution theory is the only thing that has "evolved."

The only understanding that fits perfectly with the facts is
that animals were made purposely and specifically to fit into their
respective habitats. They were created to be what they are. They
look exactly today as the day they were created. New breeds and
hybrids developed by man (who has that authority and ability)
are the only legitimate exceptions. Even then, the animals in
question did not change into another species but were simply hybrids of their kind. So, the question remains, what will animals
look like in heaven? Will they look like the animals we have here
on earth or will they be obviously different in appearance? Will
they have wings like Pegasus of Greek mythology or be some
type of spiritual, shadowy creature?

We have nothing more than a glimpse of the afterlife in scripture. As I pointed out previously, only enough is said about this
wonderful place called heaven for us to know that it is a place to
be greatly anticipated and hoped for. Perhaps a shortage of details was intended. I doubt that the lure would be so great or that
the thought would hold our imagination as powerfully as it does
if the Lord had given us every minute detail about the place.
Still, there are those who try to provide those details. I have sitting on my desk a book about heaven that I have only briefly
scanned. It is approximately four hundred pages thick with an
attractive cover. It was a gift from a friend. My initial reaction
to receiving it probably should have been "How wonderful, I
can't wait to read it," but instead, because I felt a twinge of skep-

ticism about what the book might contain, I only uttered a short thank you.

I just could not help my initial impression. The fact that it was 400 pages in length caused me some concern. If we were to type out all that the Bible says about what to expect in heaven in terms of physical beauty and activities, we might complete three or four pages of typing. So holding this large book in my hands, I was a bit wary wondering what the other 396 pages could be about.

My skepticism was justified. In just a brief scan of the text, I discovered nearly two-dozen unsupportable assumptions, three of which are very much in conflict with what scripture teaches. And frankly, some of the author's conclusions were preposterous. I am sure the man meant well as his commentary is intentionally very positive and uplifting, but he allowed his speculation to bleed over into his doctrine, and that is never a good thing. The thoughts of men can never trump the truths of God.

In light of his mistakes, I want to be careful about what I say on the topic of heaven, even in the relatively benign subtext of what our animals will look like there. There is not an abundance of direct information, so we will have to rely on those glimpses we are given to draw some dependable conclusions. In doing so, I will be very careful not to allow speculative conclusions to be more than that.

Let me begin by eliminating some potential confusion. Some references to creatures or beasts will lend nothing to our study. The information given is sketchy at best, and no conclusions can be drawn from these brief references. It is best to mention them now and get them out of the way. In one such instance, scripture refers to there being creatures around the throne of God. You can search the web and find no shortage of ideas about what these creatures may be. Except for rejecting the certifiably bizarre claims, there is just not enough said for us to know for sure who is right, if indeed anyone is. I offer my brief opinion about these creatures as nothing more than that—my opinion. My thoughts are not conclusive. There is just not enough revealed for me (or anyone) to know with absolute certainty.

Let us see what the scripture says. The creatures are briefly mentioned in Revelation 4 and 5. Let us concern ourselves with Revelation 4:6–8, which offer the best description. This passage says,

> *And round about the throne were four beasts full of eyes before and behind. And the first beast was like a lion, and the second beast like a calf, and the third beast had a face as a man, and the fourth beast was like a flying eagle. And the four beasts had each of them six wings about him; and they were full of eyes within: and they rest not day and night.*

Obviously, these creatures are unlike anything we have seen on earth, save perhaps in our nightmares or a bad sci-fi B movie. From our experiences, they indeed seem to fit more into a horror movie rather than our ideas of heaven. I do not mean to be disrespectful to God or his creatures. I merely want to frame this account in terms we can all relate to. We are only able to visualize in context with our experiences, and we have not seen creatures like this in our reality.

The actual physical attributes of multiple eyes in front and back and six wings does not describe any animal named by Adam. We also do not have evidence or knowledge of this animal. Obviously, these are unique creatures, likely made for special and specific purposes. My inclination, therefore, is to ignore this reference completely in our attempt to determine what animals will look like in heaven. Earth's animals do not look like them. In fact, I would be tempted to describe them as a special order of angels rather than animals if the Bible did not specifically call them creatures, which is a term almost always associated with animals. So I will just conclude that they are some sort of unique animal or possibly some special order of angels and let it go at that for now. I will refer to these creatures again in chapters 7 and 9, but for completely different reasons as you shall see.

Next, we have beastly references to Satan. He is referred to as a lion, beast, and dragon, to name a few. I think all will agree that these are purely figurative and have no bearing on our study. So we will spend no more time than these few lines on that.

Finally, there are other creatures mentioned that we need to eliminate from our study: creatures that come out of the earth during the great tribulation. You may read about them in Revelation 9. They are referred to as "locusts," but I believe that this too is figurative. The description offered makes them appear to be anything but locusts. They appear as horses with teeth like lions. I want to eliminate these from our study too. They are unique, and while we are told they come out of the earth, they seem to have no relation to the animals of the earth or our study.

What few animal references we do have in scripture, to either the heavenly home or the millennium kingdom, are of animals that we readily recognize (horses, lions, lambs, etc.). Admittedly, when the Bible mentions these animals, no description accompanies the reference, but that would suggest we are to assume that animals will look the same in the next life as they do here rather than imagine some differences.

Again, the Bible is aimed at humankind. Animals are not the primary focus. So in order to understand how a thing applies to animals (if indeed it applies at all), we must look at how it applies to people. In the case of what animals will look like, we must ask, what will people look like? The answer to this question is definitive. People will look the same in the next life as they do here on earth. Every instance in scripture where someone was allowed to see beyond the veil of this life, the personalities seen were recognizable (Lazarus, Abraham, Moses, Elijah, the rich man, etc.).

There will be significant differences of course. We are told that the resurrected body will be without blemish. The person will still appear the same, but its body will be without deformity, blemish, acne, scar, disease, and so on. It will also be eternal and sinless. Those are just a few of the differences. So if you are not happy with your personal appearance here, I would not worry about that; there can be no doubt but that the new body, while maintaining the same general appearance, will be glorified and beautiful. But since it will be free of the vanity of earth, I suppose it is a moot point anyway.

Applying our standard then, we have to believe animals will look the same in their new life as we humans do in ours. Do not believe otherwise. This topic is not addressed, and my experience is that if a topic is not addressed in scripture, the answer is obvious. In any event, whether animals look the same in heaven as they do on earth is not really a critical issue. Most of us are very happy just to know that God cares about them and that they will be there.

I have withheld one other piece of evidence I would like now to focus on. A time is coming known as the final millennium. This final one thousand years begins at the Lord's Second Advent, following the great seven-year tribulation. At this time, animals will be restored to their original status as companion or tame animals. We are told that all the animals will eat hay and things will be as they were in the garden. Apparently, the fear of man will be taken from the animals and we shall live in harmony. A person will be able to walk out into a field, approach a bear, and pet it without fear on either side. The child will even be able to put a hand near a venomous snake without harm. In all probability, the venomous snake will no longer be venomous.

Many things will be going on during this one thousand years, and I will be the first to admit that the restoration of animals to tame status does not register high on the scale of importance. However, just for the purpose of our study, I wanted to bring it up for one reason—animals in this period are forevermore returned to the state God wanted them to live in. The impact of the curse (the result of the fall of humankind) will have been removed, and they will be precisely and exactly as God had created them. Need I remind you that they were created to live forever? They will then be as they were created, never to be changed again.

Imagining that there would be reason for their appearance to change is baseless. When they suffered under the curse of man's rebellion, that changed them from tame vegetarians to wild meat eaters, like man himself, but their appearance did not change. There is no reason to believe that when they make the transition back to their original state that they will change either. The evidence may be circumstantial and less than overwhelming, but I think a preponderance of that evidence allows us to make a very solid case for the appearance of our animals remaining unchanged.

Chapter 6

WILL OUR PETS KNOW US IN HEAVEN?

Will our pets know us in heaven is a question calling for an assumption that there is indeed an afterlife. I have no problem making this very positive assumption, because for me heaven is a real place. There is no doubt in my mind. It is as real to me as my present reality is. This place exists right now, at this moment, and others are already enjoying it.

Another assumption is called for by this question that is not quite as positive. It touches on a topic that I find the most difficult to address when posed to me in question form by readers. Asking if our pets will know us in heaven seems to assume that we will be there for them to know or not know. I cannot answer this question either on an individual basis or in a general context.

The responsibility to know if one is right with God, and therefore has a place with him in the next life, is about as personal and individual as something can be. No one—no priest or minister; president or prime minister; mother or father—can make that determination for you. Each of us must meet God on his or her terms and are accountable only for that person.

Across the cultures of humankind, you will find no shortage of ideas on what it takes to achieve heaven, nirvana, the great beyond, or the afterlife, referred to by many other names. Everyone and his or her brother has "seen the light" in one's own respective religions or faiths. At least on this most of us can agree. For me, only one possible way is available to ensure that we can enter the afterlife and that is to meet the entry requirement set in place by the one who lives and reigns there. The requirement for entry is disclosed in the Bible. God gives us his way to effect reconciliation with him, and he says it is the only way. According to him, all else is the imagination of men. All else cannot be trusted. All else will fail.

Each of us is accountable to God to meet his standard. If we do, then we are ensured a place with him. We can safely make the assumption called for in the title of this chapter. But the key is that the choice rests in the hands of the individual and nowhere else. Only you (or I) can answer the question about our own presence in heaven one day. It is not for me or anyone else to say. However, assuming that you have made the right choice and are comfortable in the knowledge that you have guaranteed reservations, we can now focus on the question posed in the chapter's heading. Will our pets know us in heaven? Will they recognize us?

I have not found a reason to think that they will not recognize us. Once again we will have to fall back on what the Bible says about people and apply what we learn to animals, but as we have seen previously, there is no hazard in doing this. If God is nothing else, he is consistent. So we can assume that what applies for one, applies for the other. God does all things in a right way. Though humanists might disagree, there can be only one right way. God will always do all things the right way.

Very few examples can be found in scripture that will help us answer the title question, but what is available should be sufficiently convincing. First up is Luke 16:19–31. Here we have an account of an interaction between three real people in the afterlife. The players are Abraham, Lazarus, and a rich man with no name. Abraham needs no introduction as he is a prominent figure in scripture, and we consider him the example of one who has placed his faith in God. But the other two may not be as familiar to you, so allow me briefly to introduce them to you.

The rich man is described as a *certain* man, indicating that the account was of a real and specific person and not just a parable. This man was clothed regally and faired sumptuously each day. He was by today's standards well-off. It would appear that his business took him frequently through the city's gate. He was therefore very recognizable.

Lazarus, our final character in the story, was a crippled beggar who was covered in sores. He sat often, if not daily, at the gate. He was assisted by others to situate himself there each day that he might beg crumbs and alms from those who passed through, particularly the rich man. No doubt Lazarus was as recognizable to the rich man as the rich man was to Lazarus. We are not told that, but from the story it is a safe assumption.

We are told that Lazarus perished and went to paradise and was found in Abraham's bosom. Soon after, the rich man died and went to Hades, which, at that time, existed in the same place as paradise, but they were divided one from the other. Let us not concern ourselves with the differences of these two places or the reasons either went to them. Rather, let us focus on their unexpected reunion and the way it contributes to answering our question about recognition of others in the next life.

Verse 24 tells us:

> And he [the rich man] cried and said, "Father
> Abraham, have mercy on me, and send Lazarus,
> that he may dip the tip of his finger in water, and
> cool my tongue; for I am tormented in this flame."

Clearly, the rich man recognized Lazarus. He had seen him begging at the gate of the city back on earth, day after day for many months, perhaps years. He may have stopped occasionally to give him alms or food. He may have even had a conversation with Lazarus once in a while. On the other hand, the rich man may have ignored Lazarus. We simply are not told. Whatever the case, he clearly knew Lazarus by sight.

As a side issue that really has little to do with the question we are trying to answer, the next thing I note is that the rich man recognized Abraham. Abraham and the rich man had never met, for Abraham had passed away long before the rich man had been born. Later in the following verses, we also see that Abraham knew the rich man and knew of his life. These two facts are wonderful evidences of the understanding that in the next life we will have far superior knowledge and awareness than we possessed here. But again, this is another issue not for this book.

No doubt the rich man had also seen drawings of the great man of God, Abraham, and heard countless accounts of the things God did in his life. Perhaps this knowledge facilitated his recognition of the great man. No doubt, his earthly knowledge and increased afterlife knowledge worked together to help him make a positive identification.

Another example we can draw from is found in the gospels of Matthew, Mark, and Luke, chapters 17, 9, and 9, respectively. In an event labeled "the transfiguration," Jesus met with Moses and Elijah. The reason for the meeting is not specifically disclosed, but most theologians agree it was a confirmation of Jesus's Lordship to his disciples.

Regardless, our interest in the account of this miraculous event is to show that there was immediate recognition of these two giants of faith by the disciples. They had never met these men, but like the rich man's knowledge of Abraham, they had heard stories about, and perhaps seen images, of them. Their recognition of these great men, coupled with the rich man recognizing Abraham leads one to believe that in the afterlife greater knowledge of things and people will be imparted to us. In other words, we will know things, know about things, and know people we previously did not know. We can therefore safely assume that there is recognition in heaven. There can be little doubt that in the next life we will recognize those we knew on earth. Most probably we will know those we did not know because of increased knowledge. If this is so for humans, then we can safely apply this to animals and answer the question at hand. Indeed our animals will know us in heaven.

Now do not misconstrue what I am saying. I am not suggesting or do I believe that our relationship with our animals or pets will be the same as it was on earth. We will know them and they will know us. We will no doubt have minireunions with family, friends, and pets. We will rejoice to see them there and enjoy fellowshipping with them, but relationships in heaven are undoubtedly different from what they were on earth.

Heaven is a place where the focus is on God, not people, animals, angels, or any other thing. Even so, we will enjoy the friendship and fellowship of others. But it will be secondary to our fellowship with God.

Whatever heaven will be, we have the ironclad, God-given guarantee that it will be a place of bliss and happiness. No one will have cause for regret or dissatisfaction. There will be no disease, no fear, and none of the ills of earth. I do not think we could hope or ask for anything better than what God has planned for us. If the relationships we enjoyed here on earth are different in heaven, they will be better, sweeter, and Godly.

Chapter 7

ANIMAL COMMUNICATION

The topic of animal communication was addressed in more detail in *Cold Noses*. However, animal communication is such an intriguing topic, that it is worth duplicating in large part here. I do not want readers of this book to have to purchase another to enjoy the exciting possibility of animals being able to talk.

Can animals communicate? I mean, can they speak and listen like you and I? Would it not be a wonderful thing if you could one day sit down and carry on a conversation with a departed pet during your long-awaited reunion? I think everyone acknowledges that animals communicate among themselves. Dolphins "click" directions to each other and round up baitfish in an organized, concerted group effort. Wolves, birds, and animals of all sorts seem to have a system whereby they communicate with growls, grunts, chirps, and body language. One can find evidence that some animals can communicate between species.

Certain fish groom eels and sharks and are not gobbled up and consumed. These predators open their mouths when prompted by the cleaner fish and allowed access into the jaws of death with impunity. Some birds clean parasites off the backs of cows without protest from the host. And, of course, humans successfully communicate with many species of animals. But can animals communicate with us? More precisely, will animals be able to communicate with us in the next life? For some, this may not be an important issue, but I think you will enjoy hearing my speculation on the topic nonetheless.

What if animals can talk? What an amazing eventuality that would be! Could you imagine the conversation you might carry on with the cat that you haven't seen in thirty years? How shocked would you be to find out that Spot never really liked chasing that ball, and he just did it because he thought you liked it?

That I present this as speculation does not necessarily mean that I do not believe it to be a very real possibility. In fact, I believe that animals will be able to speak to humans in the next life and carry on intelligent conversations. Some very interesting indicators to consider are available in support of this.

Let us start at the beginning, the beginning of time. Let us visit back to that brief period of innocence that we know as the Garden of Eden. The devil, the Bible tells us, assumed the form of a serpent and spoke to Eve, tempting her to do something she wasn't supposed to do. Eve responded to the serpent. In fact, a short conversation took place. I am not going to recount the conversation, for that is really not important at this time. Everyone has heard the story anyway. Instead, I want to point out that the most amazing thing about their conversation was that they had one at all.

How would you react if you were in your garden and you

came across a snake and it spoke to you and said, "Okay, don't panic. . . . I know people don't like snakes, but I am harmless and you really don't need that shovel you are reaching for." I am sure it would shake you up a little. Snakes are not supposed to talk! Animals are not supposed to talk. Anyone would react with great alarm if an animal of any kind began a conversation with him or her.

However, no indication is given that Eve was at all taken aback by the serpent having the ability to speak. She did not hesitate or wince in any way. Instead, she responded to him as if it were a normal occurrence or as if it had happened many times before. Eve was not shocked. She did not react as if it were something that should shock her. She did not react like you and I would react today. The only logical conclusion is to accept that speaking was not an unexpected thing for an animal to do, but one that was normal in their innocent world.

I believe both Adam and Eve had previously talked to this serpent. It just seemed to be routine and normal for them. And it makes me wonder if the rest of the animals in the garden did not have the same ability of speech. They were made to be companions to Adam. Would it be such a long stretch of the imagination to think that God made them with the ability to converse with Adam? It is not at all out of the realm of possibilities.

The next indicator is that there are many birds that have the ability to speak: parrots, parakeets, ravens, crows, mynah birds, and others. Some might contend that their speech capability is limited, and perhaps that is true, but I have seen some birds whose abilities seem to know no limits.

A good friend of mine had a place of business where he

allowed his personal parrots to roam freely during business hours. One particular bird, an African Gray by the name of Lola, was remarkable. She could almost carry on a conversation with a person. She also had this talent for being able to duplicate sounds perfectly. She could sound like a truck warning signal, the television alert test signal, and a host of others. Her particular favorite was imitating the ring of the telephone. A portable telephone was kept in the shop, and when it rang it was always a major undertaking to find it. It was an older model that had the ringer in the base. Invariably, whoever used it would forget to put the telephone back in the base when finished using it. Consequently, when it rang it rang at the base and not in the portable component, and it was anyone's guess as to where the telephone was.

We received many telephone calls during the day, and when it rang, everyone would sort of just freeze and then start running around like the old silent movie Keystone Kops trying to remember where the phone was left last. It was always utter chaos trying to find it before whoever was calling hung up.

Apparently, Lola enjoyed hearing the telephone ring. It seemed to break up the humdrum of her day by causing an exciting flurry of activity around her perch. She seemed to enjoy watching us frantically run around searching for the funny apparatus we called a telephone. I suppose it just did not ring frequently enough for her, so in time she took it upon herself to duplicate the sound of the telephone ringing. In fact, she mastered it.

I remember clearly the day she chose to unveil this new talent to us. It was a busy day—a very, very busy day. Everyone was tied up with customers or other chores. Suddenly, the telephone rang. As usual, several employees jumped to answer it, but realizing it was not in the cradle, gave that stunned-deer-in-the headlights look and then scrambled around looking for the portable telephone.

The boss found it first, clicked it on, and said, "Hello." Then he tossed the telephone on his desk and said, "I hate practical jokes." No sooner had he thrown the telephone down than it started ringing again. He picked it up and again said hello and again tossed it down, this time cursing.

A few minutes later, it rang again and I picked it up. There was nothing but a dial tone as if someone had rung it and hung up. But something was wrong. I could not put my finger on it right away, but something felt odd. After a few moments of pondering the situation, it occurred to me that the base station of the telephone, where the ringer was housed, was to my right, but I had heard the ringing to my left. It did not take me long to figure out that the ringing sound had come from Lola. I shared my suspicions with the rest of the staff, and we decided to put the telephone down again and bait her. All eyes were on her. It did not take her long. Within a second she uttered a ring sound. She was busted! And she knew it. We put the telephone in her face and said, "Ah ha! Gotcha."

You would think that being discovered would make her stop, but it did not. She continued to perform this little trick for us several dozen more times over the next couple of days. Each time the telephone rang, we would look at her with suspicion before reaching for the telephone. That darn bird had an impeccable poker face. We fell for her ploy over and over again. She was a devious one. But we were not going to be outwitted by a bird! We had a solution. No one would answer the telephone on the first ring anymore. If it rang twice, we would know it was a legitimate call. Oh, this bird was dealing with an insurmountable brain trust now. True to the plan, when the phone rang, we waited for the second ring before answering it. Antagonistically, some of the employees would answer a genuine telephone call, cover the speaker so the caller could not hear, then turn to Lola and say, "You can't fool me today, stupid."

Something told me that it was not a good idea to provoke her, but no one said anything to those who were flaunting their temporary victory in her face. And it did not take long for my suspicions to come to fruition. Imagine our surprise when just a day or two later, the telephone rang once, than rang a second time, but when answered, there was nothing but a dial tone. We had been suckered again. Lola had learned and adapted. She had apparently understood and accepted our challenge. She learned to ring twice, and even three times, with perfect interval timing between the rings.

But here is the kicker and the part that leads to my communication theory: this time when she grinned at us with that devious *gotcha* grin, she added the words "hello stupid." It was as if she was throwing our cocky words back at us. Coincidence? I do not think so. That girl was exacting vengeance by using our own words against us. Now you may say she was just mimicking the words we taunted her with, but I am sure that she was not. She took one of the words and added it to another consciously and purposely to mock us. At least, that is the way it looked to me, and I was there. Fortunately for us, she tired of the telephone game and moved on to other tricks.

Moving on to the next indicator that animals communicate with each other. This is fact, not opinion. We see it happen before our eyes almost on a daily basis: dogs barking, birds chirping, cats hissing, and so on. It is a purposeful and directed communication. Science has documented many forms of communication between animals. Some of the methods animals employ are more complicated than others, but all are effective means of communication. Commonly, this communication comes in the form of an audible sound, but sometimes it is silent (at least to the human ear). Some creatures use a whistling sound, a series of clicks or grunts, and growls. Others, like bats, send out high-frequency sound waves that are interpreted by others with the appropriate receiving apparatus.

Whatever means are employed, there is no denying that animals communicate with each other, and that they do so effectively. Other animals know exactly what is being said to them. They react and often answer; for example, one bull elk bellowing a turf violation to an intruder will result in an appropriate response. Either the intruder will retreat or meet the challenge with a bellow of his own. So for me to say that animals "talk" is not outrageous. Talking is simply a form of communication, the audible relaying of your thoughts and intentions to another. The thoughts do not have to assume the form of words that you and I understand to qualify as talking; they merely have to be understood by the intended receiver.

The truth be known, animals are sometimes more effective

communicators than humans. Now, I did not say nor do I mean that they are more intelligent or have a vocabulary equal to ours. I merely said they are more effective at times. That is because, unlike humans, animals always communicate what they mean. There is no pretense with their speech as there sometimes is with human communication.

Often, we humans will say something that could have more than one meaning. For instance, a curious fellow employee might ask innocently "Gee I wonder how Molly got that job?" She meant exactly what was said. She was merely expressing curiosity.

Another employee, motivated by jealousy, might communicate more suggestively, with a lewd emphasis, "Yeah, I wonder what *she did* to get that job!" We witness innuendos like this all the time. In fact, we are probably guilty of them ourselves.

What we say can sometimes send different signals, but not so with animals. They are straight shooters. How many of you have ever been deceived by your cat? She purred after you stroked her, but you know she did not really enjoy it. She was putting you on to stay on your good side.

Animals simply do not lie. Now sometimes they might bluff, as in the case of a mother bear protecting her young, growling and making a mock charge. But animals do not lie or deceive. The bear is simply giving a warning. And that warning is real. There is no pretense to it. Take the warning or suffer the consequences is the message being sent. When animals communicate, they mean what they say. We could learn a lesson from them. What a better world this would be if everyone learned to speak honestly.

Even insects communicate. Some of their societal networking is so intricate and so much more efficient than ours are that one wonders how anyone could believe that we humans are intellectually superior. For goodness sake, a simple termite colony runs better than the largest city ever built, minus the crime and poverty. But I am getting off track. The point I wanted to make is that animals communicate. They speak in many ways: by their appearance or countenance, by body language, and by audibility. They speak to each other, and they speak across species lines.

Finally, pets communicate with people. In fact, most if not all animals that are associated with people communicate, or they try to communicate with them; for example, dolphins and whales have a language that is becoming increasingly more discernible by humans. They use their language very effectively among themselves. Large groups of them travel and live together in great harmony because they can speak to one another. Hunter groups work together to herd schools of fish and matriarchs protect offspring by telling them where to swim in the pod. We could enumerate many other examples of effective communication if needed.

We have managed to decode and document much of the language they use. We have managed to duplicate the sounds they employ in order to speak back to them in a language they understand. We have also elevated their communicative abilities by teaching them part of our language via visual hand signals and verbal commands. Our household pets have proven to be equal, if not superior, to our ocean mammal friends. They learn quickly to communicate their thoughts to us. I will be the first to lift an eyebrow when someone says his or her pet actually talked, but there can be no doubt that the pet appears to want to talk as if it were something it could do, or once did.

As I pen these words, my terrier is doing a little dance in front of me with her pull toy dangling from her mouth. I have no doubt what she is trying to communicate to me. She has several dances that she performs, each with a different meaning. The meaning of the dance she is doing at the moment cannot be mistaken because of the prop she has in her mouth. Did I say prop? Perhaps I should have said prompt. Either way, she is delivering her message very effectively.

I now am faced with three possible choices, one of which I must communicate back to her. I can stop what I am doing and reach for her toy, which will make her very happy but take me from my work. I can say "No, not now" and her ears will drop along with her toy and she will walk off with a very sad countenance. In fact, she will exaggerate the sadness because she knows that too communicates her feelings to me. They can be such actors.

Finally, the third choice, the one I opt for is that I can simply continue typing, which she will eventually interpret as "not now, maybe later." Either she will then curl up at my feet and wait or she will start playing by herself.

Whatever option I take, we have both effectively communicated to each other. And this type of interchange is not limited to dogs. Many if not all animals have this capacity, especially those that are domesticated. I once had a kitten that made the same demands on me as the dog I just mentioned. Her toy was a string with a small piece of cloth wadded up and tied to one end. She would actually bring it to me to try to get me to play

Am I suggesting that animals can say words? Yes and no. I've known a mynah bird who spoke words. The real question is, Do they consciously pick the words they say because they know what they mean? I honestly do not know. One could make a convincing argument either way. Let me share one made by a very dear friend of mine.

He had a very intelligent cairn terrier that he swears used words all the time. For instance, when the dog wanted to go outside to take care of business, she would sit in front of one of the family members and say "Out." They swear that the dog used the word in the same way they used it when training her as a puppy. The word uttered by the dog was a bit more drawn out so that it sounded more like ooooouuuuuuu. Obviously, the dog had trouble forming the t, but my friend swore the tone and emphasis resembled the word the family had always used. She was repeating the word she knew to mean she needed to take care of business. Of course, to keep the peace between us, I gave him a cursory uh huh and let it go at that. A talking dog indeed! I was not convinced. He tried to pursue the conversation to convince me, but I cleverly changed the subject and we never revisited it, at least not at that time.

Imagine my surprise when visiting that friend's home many years later and the same dog sat in front of me and said, "Oooou- uuu." There was no doubt in my mind that the dog was speaking to me. It was quite amazing. I half expected the dog to say,

"And I need to go now if you don't mind." Since that time, I have encountered many people with dogs, cats, and other pets, who assure me that their pets genuinely try to communicate with them. I mean the animals actually are trying to form words. I have not been as fortunate. I have had many, many pets but have never had one that talked. All my pets prefer their own tongue to that of humans. None has been bilingual. Nevertheless, their ability to communicate their thoughts and emotions to me has not been diminished. By using sounds, body language, and gestures, they have adequately communicated to me. They absolutely have the capacity to communicate to us and understand what we say to them.

The beasts or animals in heaven speak. They use audible, understood words to worship God the Father. More importantly, it appears that this is not an uncommon or unique occurrence in scripture. A serpent spoke to Eve, a donkey spoke to a prophet, and these creatures speak to God. As stand-alone facts, these accounts are not a preponderance of the evidence needed to conclude absolutely the point I am trying to make about animals speaking again in the future. But the evidence does not end there. In Revelation 5:13 we are told,

> *And every creature which is in heaven, and on the earth, and under the earth, and such as are in the sea, and all that are in them,* heard I saying *[emphasis added], blessing, and honor and glory, and power be unto him that sitteth upon the throne and unto the Lamb for ever and ever.*

One must note that portion of this verse I placed in roman type for emphasis. The Apostle John, who God used to pen this book, wrote "heard I saying." In other words, he personally witnessed the creatures speaking. They spoke. They are nonhuman creatures, most likely of the animal order, who communicated with words just like humans.

Now with that in mind, if you will study all the elements of this verse out, you can only arrive at one conclusion. Only one interpretation fits perfectly. God is saying through John that one day all created creatures of earth will one day praise God. It does not say some creatures. It does not say many creatures. It does not even say most creatures. It says *all*. We can only conclude then that *all* earthly creatures, human and animal, will have the ability to speak.

One side note on all of this please: I have learned over the years to take time to qualify the general statements I make. To ensure that I do not get an avalanche of e-mails asking me things like "When you say ALL, do you mean spiders and ants will be able to speak too?"

Whenever and wherever I use the word "creature" in relation to the next life, I am not referring to insects, amoebas, parasites, or germs. The long explanation for this is already documented in *Cold Noses*, as I am sure most of you already know, so I will not go into great detail here. Rather, let me offer a short explanation. In order for a creature to be eternal or to have an eternal soul or essence, that creature must possess a personality. The English language does not always allow for clear application of a word and that is the case here.

It would seem that the root word "person" would be applicable exclusively to humans, but that is not so. In this instance, it must also be applied to animals, for they, too, are living souls or essences as we have previously shown. They have personalities because they are individual essences. They possess emotions, cognitive reasoning, and a consciousness of more than just themselves. We can tell one animal apart from another because they consciously choose to be the individual they are. You may place the dividing line wherever you deem it appropriate in the animal kingdom. For me, insects, microorganisms, plants, and the like, are to be excluded because they lack individual personality.

CONCLUSION ON ANIMAL COMMUNICATION

Are any of these indicators that I have shared with you overwhelmingly convincing as to the ability of animals to speak? No. Independently, each thought is composed of some fact and some speculation. Individually, each fact presents a weak argument. I readily admit that.

Collectively, however, they give us considerable cause to believe that animals have the ability to speak or at least once did. These thoughts mesh together to give us a preponderance of the evidence we need. The evidence is not overwhelming, but it is very convincing. Far less evidence has been accepted to establish religious dogma on more important issues.

Whether you accept that animals once did and may once again speak, you have to admit that they do communicate. We must acknowledge their attempts to speak and be sensitive to their needs. When we keep pets, we take on the responsibility of caring for their needs and no one can tell you their needs better than they. Animals need for us to be sensitive to their attempts to communicate. When your best friend is pawing at your leg while you are watching the news, he is trying to tell you something. If they do their little dance or if they just sit in front of you and stare, probably they are sending a message. When an animal is sure that its attempts to communicate with you have been successful, it usually gives a positive reaction. They generally jump and dance around in joy and act silly. Sometimes they will actually smile.

In my opinion this reaction is not only because they have gotten what they wanted, but also because they are gleeful for having communicated to you. My pets display great pride when they have successfully "talked" to me. This benefit of being able to communicate is critical to a good and safe relationship with our pets. It is important that we listen to them. Likewise, it is fundamental that pets listen to us and understand what we are saying.

Since pets depend on us for sustenance and protection more than we rely on them for what they contribute to the relationship, we must exercise a modicum of control over their daily activities. We do that by communicating effectively to them.

While some may not care for my use of the word "control," that control is precisely what keeps them out of danger as they live in our world. Let me give you an example of what I mean: I was jogging one sunny afternoon in Miami, far outside the city in an area known as horse country. As I worked my way along a very scenic road, I noticed two Weimaraners running toward me from deep inside a very large and unfenced yard on the opposite side of the street. They were coming toward me from about two hundred feet away at a very quick pace. Although they were barking and charging, they did not appear to be a real threat. It seemed they were more bent on making the point that they were on the job than they were on the attacking. They were communicating that they were ready to defend their property from all intruders, including the dreaded jogger.

I have absolutely no fear of dogs, so I did not feel that I was in danger at all. I was more concerned about their safety than my own. They were coming on fast, and it did not appear as if they were going to stop at the property's edge, which was actually the beginning of the paved street. It was clear to me that they did not know that there was a car coming down that road at a fairly good clip, It looked to me as if it was going to arrive at their point of crossing just about the same time they did. I could do nothing to get the attention of the oncoming driver in time, so I did the only thing I could do. I stopped, faced the dogs, and yelled loudly in a very demanding and authoritative voice, "STOP!" Both dogs stopped in their tracks, almost in cartoon fashion, their legs slipping underneath them. They stopped just before reaching the asphalt road, at almost precisely the same moment the car went whizzing by. I was very relieved. The dogs looked at each other as if to say *"Man, he's mean . . . and he is on the other side of the street after all."* They then turned back toward the house and disappeared from sight, never knowing how close to tragedy they had come. I was very happy to have been of service to those animals. I am happy also that their owner had taken the time to communicate with them and teach them obedience to commands

Animals we invite to live in our world with us are subject to dangers they are usually not aware of, and listening to us is so very important. The outcome of this situation was favorable due in large part to their ability to listen, understand, and obey. I am sure this was the result of their people taking time to condition them to do so. I think about those beautiful dogs now and then and wonder if their luck is still holding. I certainly hope so.

Their story helps me illustrate my point. Animals are able to listen and understand. I am not saying that they sit around all day thinking, I hope my master tells me to roll over later, but once the request to do so is made, they remember and are able to discern what is meant. Habit or conditioning? Perhaps. However, I think it is more.

This ability that animals have to understand and respond to humans allows us to bond with and love them. Being able to communicate creates and nurtures a strong tie between those communicating.

Now I realize that there are exceptions. Some pets do not possess that capacity and we bond with them anyway. Reptiles, amphibians, and fish, for instance, do not communicate with humans in the true sense of the word as we have used it in this study. Through repetition, they may know when it is time to eat, and they become more active and responsive at those times. They may even recognize or actually tolerate the presence of one human over another. Their apparent excitement and their ability to distinguish the difference in people are due to the sustenance they anticipate rather than the preference of one person to another.

Do they love us? As an amateur herpetologist, with much experience in the field of reptiles and amphibians, I am compelled to say that they do not. We certainly get attached to them. We certainly grieve their passing. But we do not hold them in as high regard as a pet that can reciprocate our affections and communicate its love for us.

Even the iguana, which enjoys one of the best reputations for cohabitation with humans, falls far short of the capacity of some of what we consider the lowliest of mammals. Take for instance, the domestic rat. To most people these little gray, tan, and white mammals are not much different from their wild cousins who scour the sewers and garbage heaps for a living. Rats are seen as nasty, disgusting creatures. Most people would prefer to keep a toad than a rat. I admit they are not very clean animals and sometimes they can be mean, inflicting nasty bites. I have been on the receiving end of their incisors on many, many occasions. They are defensive, and if not accustomed to close human contact, they can and will bite.

More frequently, however, domestic rats are friendlier than most people think. Social creatures by nature, they fit very well into our world as pets, very much like a cat or dog. The inherent problems are that they do not readily housebreak, they have poor hygiene, and their life expectancy is short. Allowing children to keep them as pets can prove to be rewarding but also traumatic as their life expectancy is shorter than other domestic animals. Still, many people swear by them as good pets. They can show affection and respond to commands. They are loyal creatures that have been known to defend their people from per-

ceived threats. I knew one little girl who had a wonderful relationship with her pet rat. She bathed it and groomed it and taught
it tricks. They became very close. It even slept at the foot of her
bed each night in its own little bed. While the little girl slept,
the otherwise peaceable creature would not let anyone but the parents near the little girl without strong protest, not even the family
dog. This action communicated its intention to guard the little
girl very clearly.

The point is that those pets that we surround ourselves with
(and I speak of mammals and birds almost exclusively in this
section) listen to us, sometimes intently. They learn to respond
to commands and requests by repetition, but they can also understand and respond appropriately to things that they hear for
the first time.

Undoubtedly, the perception level depends on the individual
animal. I suspect they are like people in that regard. Some of us
are less intelligent than others. Some of us focus on different in-
terests so that we are highly motivated by some things but slow
to show interest in others. The average household pet is no different. Some things bore them, while others hold great interest.
Their attention level is commensurate with their interest level.

Animals may no longer possess the ability to speak, if in fact
they ever had it at all, but they do still listen and understand.
Their level of understanding may vary from animal to animal,
but when an animal bonds with people, it most certainly pays
attention when those people communicate with it. Some focus so
passionately on listening that we feel inclined to hold complete
conversations with them.

Cats are prone to sit and listen to their humans for long periods of time, and they often show great interest in what is being
said. Readers report to me that their cat will purr when they are
telling them about a pleasant experience or swish their tail the
way cats do when they speak of something that is bothersome to
their human friend. They seem to understand. Some may attribute this to a reaction by the animal to voice inflections, but
that is too convenient an explanation. There is much more substance to its reaction than a perception of mood. If it were just
that, it would be evident only at the moment of exchange, but
often the family pet's mood will mirror the prevailing mood in
the family unit for long periods. Your world overlaps its world.
What upsets you upsets the pet.

I had one wonderful old cat who would listen so intently that
I thought he was going to answer me. When I sounded glad, he
seemed glad, and when I was in an apparent bad mood, he too
seemed agitated. I know he somehow perceived my mood and
reacted to it, but as anyone who has kept cats knows, they also
understand our words. They relate to what is going on with us.
They tap into our lives and become an active part of it. Their
perception is amazing. They are intelligent and perceptive creatures. Both cats and dogs possess great ability to understand their
people. Certainly, they learn much through repetition, but it is
clear that they can also follow simple directions in things previously not experienced.

Now I am sure you understand that this does not mean that
we can say to them *"Please go get my blue socks for me, third
drawer of my dresser in the third room down the hall"* and expect

them to be successful. There is a limit to their capacity. However, when we say go or come, most pets, be they dogs, cats, horses, birds, and so on, already know what is expected. They listen, my friend, and they understand. If you do not know or believe that, you probably do not spend enough time with your pet, and shame on you.

Chapter 8

DO ANIMALS BECOME ANGELS?

If there is one subject that seems to transcend denominational borders to capture the collective interest of all of Christian persuasion, it is this topic of angels. People like to talk and hear about angels. You will find no shortage of ideas about what they look like and what their purpose is. There also is an abundance of accounts of encounters with them.

While I will briefly touch on those things in this chapter, I am not going to spend much time in the details. I only want to spend enough time to build a foundation on the history and function of angels so that we can answer the question at hand, namely, do animals become angels when they pass on to the next life?

In this chapter, I will be speculating on some thoughts I have regarding a possible animal / angel connection, and that I hope will provoke you into developing and exploring new ideas of your own. My speculation will be intermingled with fact, and I will labor to ensure that the distinction is clear. Please make sure you do not try to build a factual case on things I speculated about.

An important rule to apply when discussing biblical things is that extreme caution should be exercised to ensure that speculation is labeled as such and not blindly accepted as fact or doctrine. When this rule is not followed, speculation eventually evolves into accepted doctrine, which is how cults take root. I never want to be guilty of passing on my personal speculation as fact or do I want anyone to do so for me. I will be thinking out loud for the reader, sharing some of the thoughts I have entertained regarding the possible connection between animals and angels. Some of my thoughts will undoubtedly cause lifted eyebrows, but please frame them in the context in which they are offered; they are merely possibilities. My studies continue and I have not yet arrived at the point where I can re-label my speculations as conclusions.

It may sound as if I were about to reveal some extraordinary, previously unknown facts about angels that will set the world of religion on its ear, but that is not the case. I merely am going to answer the question posed by the chapter heading and attempt to show a connection between animals and angels. It is the same question that many, many readers have posed to me over the years and it is the same answer I have given them.

My intention is not to be flippant or irreverent in what I present. I simply want to share ideas. We all speculate on spiritual things (where God came from, who created him, etc.). No disrespect to God is intended. No damage is done. It is human nature to wonder and speculate. And that is all I am doing in this chapter, wondering and speculating.

Let us begin by acquainting ourselves with angels. This will not be a detailed study, just an overview to help us all get on the same page. We all have different ideas about angels and what they are. Some view them as superheroes, and perhaps at times they are. Some consider them guardian or guarding beings, and again at times they are. Some think that angels are just humans who have passed on. Others disagree with that. There are literally myriad ideas about who these beings are and what they do. So I think we must biblically define what an angel is. And do not worry, I am not going to load you down with a lot of scripture but mostly just paraphrase what is said.

According to the Bible, angels are created beings. They were created to serve God and to fellowship with him long before humans and animals ever were a reality. They are genderless and do not procreate. They are eternal creatures who do not die. As a consequence, the same number of angels exist today as there were the day they were created. Obviously then, angels are not departed humans who have been given their wings, as one old cliché speculates.

I remember in the movie *It's A Wonderful Life*, the little girl in the family had a line that lent credit to this misconception. A bell tinkled in the movie and the little girl said something like "Someone else has gotten their wings, daddy," meaning of course that someone had passed away and become an angel.

As cute and moving a thought as that is, it is whimsical and not factual. Humans do not become angels when they pass on to the next life or at any other time, for that matter. You can search the Bible from cover to cover and never find support for that notion. Angels are completely separate creatures from humans. They are not made in God's image. They are not triune beings as we are. They are the messengers of God as we will see later in this chapter.

It is likely that the idea that humans become angels came from the fact that scripture tells us that angels can take human form in their service to God. This is undoubtedly true. They can and do take human form and visit the earth. That does not make them human. It only makes them pass as human. We had a young man dress up as a bear at Coast Guard Academy games. This did not make him a bear. He only looked like one. Angels can take human form or dress up to look like humans, but they are still angels. And for the record, it does not work the other way; people do not become angels. Like angels, we are eternal, but we are eternally human.

Angels were separated into three main groups. seraphim, cherubim, and archangels. Archangels are probably members of the cherubim order, but no one is certain, so we will just make them a third order. All angels from these groups are the servants of God, but each has a specific role they fill in the heavenly order. A fourth group developed because of the rebellion that Lucifer led against God with approximately one third of the angels. These are now called fallen angels or demons.

There are websites that report up to nine orders of angels, but this is erroneous. At times in scripture we are told about special groups of angels (such as in the book of Revelation) that are assigned special tasks. These special groups are not a separate order, but just members of one of the aforementioned groups separated to do a special, temporary job. There are exceptions even to this rule, such as the creatures around the throne that we previously discussed in chapter 4. These are described to be physically

different from the others, but not enough is known for us to consider them a separate order. They may not even be angels, although I believe they are.

Angels were used to do God's bidding. If you are familiar with
the Bible, you will know that angels were the heralds who, along
with God's select prophets and judges, declared the edicts and
thoughts of God to his people. Angels are the ones who approached Lot in Sodom and Gomorrah. An angel told Joseph
that Mary was with child. Angels are the ones who announced
the birth of Christ to the shepherds. They were the messengers
of God. The roles of angels are many, and a study in this area is
recommended to all. You will undoubtedly find it very interesting. There are any number of good books, and I heartily recommend you find the time to read one if you want to understand
all that the Bible has to say about these beings known as angels.
For our purposes, however, I want to focus on only two roles of
angels: that of guardianship and ministering. In fact, these roles
are so closely related to each other, you may detect no difference
between them as I refer to them.

I promised I would not quote too much scripture in this book,
but citing some select verses here is necessary and I beg your in-
dulgence. In the book to the Hebrews 1:14, we find the following rhetorical question about angels:

> *Are they not all ministering spirits, sent forth to*
> *minister for them who should be heirs of salvation?*

The first thing that you must see is that angels were *sent forth*.
They do not wander around aimlessly throughout creation look-

ing for things to do. They have order and discipline. God knows where they are at all times and purposely sends them to minister. They are doing his bidding. They are to be ministers or care givers to those "who should be heirs of salvation." Who are these heirs? They are simply God's children. They are those who are called by his name or Christians.

The words "should be heirs" is in the future tense, but it applies to both the future and the present. Those of us who have accepted the Son of God as savior are immediately and currently heirs of salvation, but we will not actually realize the inheritance until either we pass from this life or the Lord comes back for us as we discussed previously. The inheritance is like a trust fund. It belongs to the person who owns it but is not realized until that person comes of age. Coming of age for the Christian translates to passing from this life. Our inheritance is a heavenly trust fund if you will. It is ours. No one can take it from us. But we must wait until we come of age to realize it completely. We know about it now. We look forward to getting it. We tell others about it and claim our status as heir to the king. But we must wait until we come of age to receive it.

The verse also says that angels are "ministering" spirits. What exactly does that mean? To be sure, it does not mean that they are to be put on a pedestal or worshiped in any way as some have done. It does not mean that they can be priest over men and women in any sense of the word as others have attempted to do. This is strictly forbidden by God (see Colossians 2:18 and Revelation 22:8–9). Also, the verse does not translate to suggest that they are to be our servants where they do our bidding. Angels do God's bidding only, and he equips them with great power and ability to accomplish his will. This may not be exactly theologically accurate, but in a way God uses them as extensions of himself to do his will. He sends and they do. They serve God, not humankind. How they serve God is to minister to God's children.

Their ministering nature speaks of their being guardians of the heirs of salvation. Perhaps it would be more accurate and certainly clearer if I said guards rather than guardians. Theirs is not to be responsible for the actions of Christians, as would be expected of a guardian. Rather, they are to watch over us, to guard or protect us as God directs them to. How do they guard us, and to what degree? I am not sure that anyone is able to answer this question fully. In all probability, there are so many angels and so many ways they have exercised their protective roles, that it would be impossible to discover let alone enumerate them all. At other times, when bad things befall us, we wonder if there are any around at all. But they are. They are doing God's will, not their own, and they are ever on the job.

Generally speaking, they operate in a clandestine manner to secure the safety of believers. But our awareness that they were on the job usually comes after the fact, long after they are no longer active. Let me illustrate what I mean with a true story about a very good friend of mine, a very dedicated Christian man named Gordon.

Gordon was taking his family for a drive in their new automobile. They had just maneuvered onto an access ramp to a major freeway, when suddenly the engine died. There were no warning lights or alerts. The automobile engine had not made odd noises; it just shut down for no apparent reason. Reacting quickly, he fought against the disengaged power steering and brought his car to a safe stop on the shoulder of the road. He gave his wife an exasperated look and sat for a moment as he decided what to do next. He confided in me that he was rather perturbed by the whole thing, but he did not let it show. He decided the family outing was not going to be ruined by something this minor. Gordon lived by the philosophy "We may not be able to control the things that happen to us, but we can surely control how we react to them."

Instead of getting out of the car to check under the hood (an act many of us men perform to give the appearance we know something about engines when we do not), Gordon sat for a few minutes assuring his family that everything would work out. After three or four minutes, he tried to start the engine again. To his relief, it fired up on the first try and responded to all the controls. He looked at his wife and made a shrugging motion indicating he had no idea what had been wrong or why the engine suddenly worked again. Then he put the car in gear and moved back into traffic on the on-ramp.

The on-ramp was only about a quarter of a mile long, and they should have made the freeway in no time, but there seemed to be some sort of commotion ahead on the road slowing traffic. As they neared the apparent cause of the traffic congestion, Gordon slowed down. It was obvious that it was a very bad accident. As he moved forward cautiously, he could see that there were many injuries and perhaps fatalities. He thought to stop and offer help, but there seemed to be too many people helping already. He would have stopped if his help was needed, but was relieved it was not as it was a very gruesome scene, and he did not want to expose his children to it.

As the people who had jumped out of their cars to help directed him around the worst of the wreckage, Gordon turned pale. He could see enough of the mangled mass of metal to know that it had once been the vehicle he had seen in his rearview mirror directly behind him on the access ramp prior to his engine trouble. He realized that if he had not had the engine trouble, he would not have pulled over and stopped. He would have continued down the on-ramp and entered traffic at precisely the place the car behind him had. It would likely have been his car that was mangled and his family who would have been injured or killed. Gordon was convinced that his guardian, or rather guarding angels, had intervened. I have no reason to doubt it.

This does not mean that angels protect every believer from every potential danger in every situation. Quite the contrary is true. Many believers die prematurely. Believers lose limbs, are crippled in accidents, and suffer in all the same ways nonbelievers do. Sometimes, for whatever reasons, God withholds his ministering angels from intervening. When they do intervene, however, it is always on behalf of God's children and at the discretion and direction of the Father. And they intervene in many and various ways.

To show the diverse ways that guarding angels may intervene for God's people, let me share a few scriptures. I will not recount them here, but rather give you the addresses so that you can look them up at your leisure. There are many others, but these should make my point. In Psalm 35:4–5, we see angels can harass our enemies on our behalf. In Psalm 34:7 and Isaiah 63:9, they have the ability to deliver us from evil people. In Acts 5:17–20, they rescue believers from prison. In Daniel 6:20–23, they shut the mouths of the hungry lions so Daniel, a believer, would remain safe. In 2 Kings 6:15–17, we have one of the greatest accounts of supernatural protection, where an entire army of angels was sent to protect the Prophet Elisha and his servant from those who sought to harm them. And there are myriad other examples we will not take time to mention.

Today for reasons we have previously discussed, these angelic beings usually do their work unseen by those they are guarding. Sometimes, however, they take human form to accomplish their God-directed work. Even then, we may see them, but not realize until after they depart, that they were messengers from God. We know this from what it says in the book written in Hebrews 13:2 in the New Testament, in which it says,

Be not forgetful to entertain strangers: for thereby
some have entertained angels unawares.

Isn't that a sobering thought that you may have talked to or had dealings with an angel disguised as a human being? When my daily reading brings me back to this book and verse, which is usually once every couple of years, I like to stop and think of the times and instances when an angel might have been present in my life to help me, and there have been many. Somehow, remembering those times in light of this passage makes my faith well up inside of me, a feeling similar to a patriotic rush when one of our athletes wins the gold at the Olympics.

Now for the purpose of our study, please read that verse again. It does not say conclusively that the angels are in human form. No doubt that is what it means, but the wording does not exclude the possibility that angels can take on animal form as well. Is it possible that angels also appear as animals to walk among us and perform their work of protection? There are not many examples available to us in scripture to show that angels can occupy the bodies of animals, but there are examples:

- 🐾 The account of the Lord casting out the demons named Legion from the maniac—they asked to be able to enter a herd of swine and were given leave to do so.
- 🐾 Satan assuming the form of a serpent in the Garden of Eden.

I must admit that these are not very good examples by which to make my point that angels can take animal form, but they do show that not only is it possible, but it has happened. Despite the absence of additional specific examples, however, we do have many instances where animals were used of God to serve him or his purposes. For example, the ravens that fed the prophet, the she-bear who exacted judgment for the mocking of a prophet, the mule that spoke, the great fish that swallowed Jonah, and so on. In this regard (and this is of key importance), animals are similar to the angels, who are used of God for special service to perform his will.

Angels historically have done God's bidding. When something needed to happen, when something needed to be revealed, or when something needed to be heralded, he usually employed his angels. The exception to this was when he used his prophets, judges, and animals. It is not a long stretch, therefore, to imagine that when animals are used of God, they are serving in the same capacity as angels. They are therefore, effectively, and for all practical purposes, agents or messengers of God just like the angels.

If you are on board with what I have said thus far, then it is just a short jump to accept that angels are able to assume animal form when it serves the purpose of God. If they can serve as guarding angels in human form, why can they not serve in animal form when the occasion calls for it? I personally believe they can and do. Is it merely coincidence that animals are often reported to have protected their people in extraordinary ways that we would not expect? I do not think so. Certainly, I will concede that some animals are bred and taught to serve in protective capacities, such as the Doberman and German shepherd. In addition, some animals protect us without even realizing they are doing so. The family cat will exercise its natural inclination to catch and dispatch mice, unconsciously protecting the family from rodent-borne diseases. A large dog, merely by its presence, might cause a thief to go to another neighborhood. But I think you know that those examples are not the types of protective acts I am referring to. Rather, I speak of those acts of protection that are outside the realm of normal behavior for an animal, where animals perform extraordinary feats and services.

Over the years I have heard similar accounts of how the family dog finds and cares for a lost child in the wilderness. How many times have we heard of cats, dogs, or birds warning the sleeping family of intruders, fire, or carbon monoxide? What of the dogs that have knocked children from the paths of cars or pulled them from lakes, risking their own safety for the good of the child?

Lest we forget the barnyard heroes, what of the horses, hogs, goats, cows, and other animals that have performed extraordinary feats of protection not only for their people but for other animals as well. There are many books and television shows celebrating our animal friends' achievements in this area.

One example that I have used before in other writings happened in the town I was living in. Briefly, a horse had fallen through the ice on the farm pond and could not get out. The situation was so desperate that only the snout of the poor creature was visible above the waterline. The horse's eyes were even below the water, and it had pushed off the bottom just to see clearly and to cry out with a whinny. With the thicker ice forbidding its exit from the pond, the horse was in great trouble. While it gasped for air, its sibling of over twenty years ran to the farmer, who was working in the barn a considerable distance from the pond. Somehow the horse convinced the farmer to follow her back to the pond. Once on scene, the farmer realized immediately what had happened and quickly mounted a successful rescue. All I can say is what you are probably already thinking, "Amazing!"

These animal heroes are not just relegated to the barnyard. We must include those creatures we consider wild as well. Some of them are to be praised for feats of protection and help. For instance, the woman lost at sea off the coast of the Philippine Islands who was rescued by a huge seagoing turtle (also mentioned elsewhere). Adrift at sea after a boating accident, she could not see land or vessels. Suddenly, a large turtle surfaced and swam toward her. She reached out and grabbed hold of the turtle's shell and held on for nearly fifteen hours. As a sailor, I can assure you that turtles do not usually behave this way toward human beings or do they remain exposed on the surface of the water for very long. This was an extraordinary situation.

Late in the day a vessel appeared on the horizon, and the turtle began swimming toward it. Witnesses on board the vessel swear to the following: that the turtle swam deliberately toward the vessel; that when the vessel stopped, the turtle swam around the vessel several times until a ladder / platform was lowered; and that the turtle swam directly to the platform where the woman was helped on board. After depositing his precious cargo, the turtle immediately sounded (dove) into the depths and was not seen again. The turtle could have submerged at any time but did so only after serving as a flotation device for several hours until the woman was safe in the hands of rescuers. Moreover, it did everything needed to affect the rescue, from waiting for a vessel to appear to waiting for the ladder to be lowered.

I am not sure of the year or newspaper at this late date, but if you care to research the story for authenticity, it was reported in either the *Honolulu Star-Bulletin* or *Honolulu Advertiser*, circa 1967–68. I was living there at the time and remember the facts of the story vividly.

Another account that was perhaps more widely disseminated by the media was the care given by a gorilla to a young toddler who fell into an exhibit at a major zoo. A large female gorilla cuddled the lad, protected him from the tomfoolery of adolescent male gorillas, and stroked the lad in an attempt to comfort him in his semiconscious state. When it came time to give him up to the curator, she acted as if she knew what to do and readily and gently passed him over.

So very many documented instances are on record describing

how domestic and wild creatures assumed the role of protector or rescuer on behalf of people. I could list a dozen or more from memory if there were room to do so, but there is not. Nevertheless, I feel I am doing these noble creatures a gross injustice by not listing as many heroic feats as I am able to. So do not be surprised if I slip a few more stories in before the end of the book.

Their service to people does not end with rescues, at least not conventional rescues. We have an emerging medical phenomenon developing regarding animal abilities that is simply mind-boggling. I am not qualified to give you any technical information, but nothing prevents me from telling you what I have learned through the media. Animals are able to diagnose potentially fatal diseases. They are able to rescue people in a way no one could have imagined, and I am sure evolution theorists could never explain. Several dogs and cats are being used to detect heart problems and cancer. According to the documentary I was viewing and a wealth of Internet information I was able to locate, doctors believe that people with certain ailments produce a chemical or hormone that dogs can detect. Some cats are able to do the same thing.

Their keen sense of smell is able to register the very minute traces of those chemicals or hormones when they are present in the human body. I suppose much like a polar bear can smell seals through thick ice. With training of both the dog and medical professionals, certain reactionary behavior by the dog (and sometimes the cat) signals a positive hit on the heart ailment or cancer in the subject suspected of suffering from it.

One of the illustrations they used was the case of a man whose dog detected each of his three heart attacks *before* he had them.

What is more, the same dog reacted to a co-worker of that man when the dog came into contact with him by chance while visiting the office. The co-worker did not take the dog's "hit" seriously. Within a short period of weeks, that man suffered a heart attack. Fortunately, he survived.

As fantastic as these documented cases are, I do not find a dog's keen sense of smell so surprising. A canine's superior olfactory ability is a well-established fact. Feats accomplished by these animals using their fantastic sense of smell are commonplace. What does surprise me is how these dogs know to react to what they are detecting in a way that warns discerning doctors that something is medically wrong. How does a dog know what cancer or heart disease smells like? I wasn't even aware that there was a distinct odor. How do they know to react to it so that people understand something is wrong? Doesn't that appear to you to be beyond the realm of their intelligence and understanding? It's certainly beyond mine, and I think that I'm at least as smart as my dog!

Animals sometimes possess discernment beyond their abilities. Perhaps that is why we are so inclined to believe that they have some sort of sixth sense and assign a measure of supernatural perception to them. Certainly, an ability of such scope and accuracy as to detect disease deep within a person's body requires more than just the sense of smell. Would that not require an insight and supernatural ability akin to what we would imagine an angel might have, working as the agents of God? I do not know the answer. I am just thinking out loud again, but this topic is so intriguing. Whatever the case, there is more to this story than we are seeing.

Now then, let us frame all that was covered just now in context with some of the things we know about angels. Certain similarities cannot be ignored. To be sure there are also many differences, but let us put those aside for the moment and focus on apparent similarities to see if a bonafide connection between angels and animals is there. I am not asking you to draw any conclusions, especially since I have not done so myself. I merely want you to consider the similarities and possibilities.

To begin, God created angels as eternal creatures. He made them with the intent that they would serve his will, which often manifests itself in their serving humankind's best interest. As the Father, God's will toward his children's well-being is that they should be safe. Angels are assigned the responsibility of guarding them. Coincidentally, God created animals as eternal creatures. They are to serve humankind, and we have already seen that this often manifests itself in their guarding or protecting us. This appears to parallel the responsibilities of angels.

Angels are not to be passive in this task, but proactive. They often do great things that are sometimes misconstrued as "miracles," but they are to do so without official recognition or fanfare. We often give them credit, but they never step forward to receive accolades for their work. So, too, animals have assumed the responsibility of guarding humans. Often they are very proactive, perhaps too much so (growling dogs, etc.). They, too, serve without expectation of reward or recognition.

Angels are empowered by God to be able to have great strength and abilities. Some of the things we have given them credit for obviously required such abilities. Might we consider the sniffing out of cancer cells by a dog or the perception of a sea turtle to recognize the need to carry a woman until a ship arrived as powers that are beyond these creatures' abilities or that are supernatural like an angel's?

There is more. Neither angels nor animals are in need of redemption. They have no need for reconciliation with God because they are sinless creatures. I know the sin of the fallen angels will come immediately to mind. Indeed, they are sinful and they are fallen, but judgment for them has already been pronounced. They are dead in that sin, and no reconciliation is possible for them. But not so for those who did not follow the devil; they are sinless, like our animal friends.

If we discount the fallen angels who left their first estate, the similarities between the faithful angels and animals are just too close to be coincidental. The parallels are too perfect for there not to be a connection that transcends our knowledge of them. I am certainly not suggesting that animals are angels in the way we understand angels. The angelic host mentioned in scripture is composed of the orders of angels we mentioned earlier. But I cannot rule out that animals could be a special order of angels called creatures. It is just a label. It is not definitive. I merely see animals as messengers that often do the things that angels are responsible to do. I see similarities in their makeup and order. I cannot prove a case with available scripture, but my mind feels a connection can be found that we are not seeing.

The creatures around the throne of God are not called angels, and yet they possess angellike qualities and responsibilities. Are they angels or creatures? Are they a hybrid of both? I do not know. All I do know is that they appear to be angelic, but they do not fit into any of the orders of the angels we know about.

The same is an applicable observation for animals. There are identifiable differences, but so many similarities are evident that they are hard to ignore.

So while I know that I cannot prove animals are an angelic order, I know that I cannot disprove it. This is one of those things we cannot know, no matter how badly we want to, no matter how hard we strive to find answers. And to be honest, even at the risk of minimizing the importance of this chapter, it really is not a very important issue. If it were, God would have given us more details. But he did not.

That then was my long answer to the question: will my pet become an angel? While they do not become angels, there is reason to believe they are already an order of angels in a very loose application of the word. They serve man and God. They are messengers or guardians of humankind. They therefore perform the role of an angel in that regard.

Previously, when direct guidance was not to be found on animals, I could correctly defer to what the Bible says about humans and apply the same principle to animals. This situation is a bit different. The Bible clearly teaches that humans do not become angels, but animals might already be, so in that sense, the same principles cannot apply. The question still remains, are animals angels? I do not know. I think there is much to consider, and whether in the end God says they were or were not will not surprise me either way. It is not a critical issue, just one of interest. What is critical is that readers understand all that I say in this chapter on this topic are my personal thoughts and speculation and nothing more. My hope is that my thoughts might provoke others to consider the possibilities with an open mind, but that no one would build some half-cocked doctrine upon it.

This false doctrine has happened all too many times with scripture, from the gap theory in Genesis 1 to the ridiculous belief derived from Genesis 6 that Nephalim (the offspring of angels and human women) exist. I do not wish to be the cause for any false beliefs like this. This is often how pseudo-Christian organizations or cults are started. Someone comes up with a revolutionary idea about God and his dealings with humankind and justifies it by pulling out some obscure word from a verse or by misrepresenting what a verse says. All of a sudden you have a cult complete with false doctrine and a following of people with itchy ears.

Accordingly, please accept my speculation for what it is—speculation. I see a connection between animals and angels that makes me wonder if animals aren't just another order of angels or perhaps directed by angels to serve and protect humankind. When God created animals, could they have just been another type of angelic being put in the garden to coexist with people, to help us on our journey through this life? My speculation is nothing more than that, nothing heretical, nothing revolutionary.

Please follow me closely here, for this is the cornerstone of my thinking. God is omniscient, of this there can be no doubt. He knows all and sees all, past, present, and future. What if, in his omniscience, looking forward to the hard life that humankind would face because of the fall in Eden he preposted another angelic order of creatures here with us to help us cope and endure? What if God simply called this other order of angels creatures?

Before you label me a nut or heretic, let me ask you this: If when you finally get to ask God about it and he says, "Why yes they were a type of angel," what consequence would there have been? None! It would not have changed a thing. It is just a label. They remain the creatures they are, enjoying the same status with God and man that they had before I asked the question. Given all this, would it not then be possible for angels and animals sometimes to work in concert with each other to the benefit of people? Remember, we are speaking exclusively of the role of guardian and are not concerned with any other capacity in which angels may serve. Angels are sent to minister to us. Animals obviously do that in many ways. I fail to see a significant difference in their roles. And even if my hypothesis is in error, at the very least I believe that guarding angels use animals to assist them in their responsibilities to protect humankind. It seems to me that this would explain a lot of the coincidences and peculiar things that happen.

In the final analysis, there just is not enough said in scripture to know for sure, so we are just going to have to wait. The good news is that it really is not that important. Most of us are happy to know that our best friends are "safe" in their creator's care and that we can see them again.

Chapter 9

THE SIXTH SENSE

W e have all heard someone claim, or claimed ourselves, that animals possess a sixth sense. That is, we hold that they possess a sense that is more than seeing, more than hearing, more than tasting, more than smelling, and more than feeling. And more often than not, we give this so-called sixth sense a supernatural flavoring, assigning an ability to the animals to know or perceive things beyond what we humans could possibly know or perceive with the five senses we possess.

This sense effectively assigns them a supernatural superiority to humans. Somehow they know the unknown. They can see things we cannot see, feel things we cannot feel. Some even allow that they may be able to see into the future, reacting physically to a phenomenon that has not yet occurred, such as an earthquake, flood, or the impending passing of another animal or human being. I do not hold to this theory. Discounting the hype of Hollywood movies and specials, I have not observed any evidence to support this view, and I have been around animals, domestic and wild, all my life. Probably more importantly, I see nothing to support such a view in the Bible, the standard I use to measure just about everything that matters in life.

From a practical standpoint, if animals possessed such ability, the impact on the animal kingdom would be nothing short of chaotic. If animals had that kind of perceptive sense, prey would never be taken because they would always know exactly where and when danger was lurking and avoid it. Conversely, predators would never miss their mark because they would only pounce when they knew they would be successful. Since these premises are mutually exclusive, that is, unable to be true at the same time—if one were true, the other could not be. Both prey and predator continue to flourish all over the globe. Destruction of habitat and pollution are taking their toll on the environment, but the impact is equally hurtful to both prey and predator. A sixth sense is simply not evident in the animal kingdom.

I have heard television personalities allude to this sixth-sense theory many times while discussing animal behavior on their shows. Invariably they make comments about these seemingly supernatural abilities of animals without offering much evidence to substantiate their claims. I could be wrong, but it seems to me that they use the phrase "sixth sense" almost as a come-on to attract the interest of the viewer. Then they abandon that claim and spend the rest of their allotted time speaking about how animals often have heightened senses and how those heightened senses, and not some other unknown ability, give them an acute awareness of their surroundings.

This whole idea of a sixth sense is a myth, an urban legend. It is a fiction that one generation passes on to another as fact. It is readily accepted and passed on because it contains a measure of sensation and mystique. Somewhere in our past it was passed on to us, and we found it an intriguing idea. We subconsciously accepted it and stored it away in our memory. Then when we subsequently witness an incredible act by an animal, we call that memory out of storage and add a little of our own spin to it to spice it up a bit, thereby doing our part to perpetuate the myth. It is nothing to be ashamed of. We all do it. We all have a bit of "fisherman yarn" inside of us. Life can be rather dull when we can explain everything that happens, and so we spice it up. Most of us like the exciting more than the ho hum. We prefer color to black and white.

So then when we combine our love for the sensational with our propensity for stretching the truth, we can sometimes draw the wrong conclusions and help perpetuate myth. That is how this business of animals having a sixth sense has come to be so accepted. It started as a passing thought, someone added meat to it, others spiced it up, and now we have a master race of animal achievers and prognosticators. When a horse rears up and acts strange for no apparent reason, well there must be an earthquake coming. When a parakeet stops chirping, there must be a bad storm approaching. When a dog howls, someone is about to die.

Most of us remember the psychological exercise conducted back in grade school that was designed to show students the life cycle of a rumor. The teacher would tell a student a purposely dull story and then ask him or her to think about it for a moment and pass the story on to the next student. That student would then pass it on to someone else, who would pass it on to someone else, and so on, throughout the entire class. The teacher would then ask the student who heard the story last to stand and tell everyone what he or she was told. Then the teacher would share the original story with the class, and everyone would have a good laugh about how the facts changed. Almost everyone added something to the story to help it along.

I submit to you that the same principles and dynamics are at work when it comes to this perpetuation of the thought that animals have a supernatural sixth sense. I do not believe that anyone is an expert in animal behavior, and I am certainly not claiming to be. But in my opinion, animals possess nothing more than the five senses of sight, hearing, taste, smell, and touch that you and I enjoy.

I will be the first to admit that sometimes animals seem to know things before they happen, but the emphasis is on the word "seem." It only appears that way, and appearances can often be deceiving. For instance, I watched a documentary about explosions on television not too long ago. As the demolition crew brought down this structure, the dozens of pigeons perched on the ledges of the building seemed to lift off the building and flee just before the explosion. Although the documentary was not about animals, the demolition experts took a few moments to review the videos they had taken to explore the sixth-sense angle of the pigeons' reaction. They were certain that the evidence would show that the birds had responded to the explosion before it actually happened. As expected, in the film taken by the demolition experts from a spot far removed from the explosion site, it appeared that the pigeons had lifted off the ledge just before the explosion.

This seemed to be proof positive that animals have a supernatural perception. If you had seen the film, you would undoubtedly agree. Not so fast. The demolition crew had also positioned cameras very close up to the building to review their work and possibly learn more about explosions. When they reviewed these videos, the flashes from the charges were seen microseconds before the first pigeon stretched its wings. This showed clearly that the birds were reacting to the explosion, not exercising some sixth-sense perception of impending danger.

Let me explore this subject just a bit further. Some assign another name for this supernatural sense. They call it instinct. In the strict sense of how this word is defined, I agree, animals possess instinct. By that I mean animals have certain skills and activities they perform that were not learned. These are just part of the life package they have from their creator. For instance, a bird building a nest, a groundhog digging a burrow, or a mother feeding her young, these are true instincts. These are, in my opinion, God-given abilities necessary for these creatures to survive.

On the other hand, I do not subscribe to the liberal interpretation of the word "instinct," or the idea that animals have some special abilities that they have developed and passed on from generation to generation. Humans can do this. We acquire knowledge and skills that we can pass on to our offspring or that they can learn from historical records. For instance, if I learn to sculpt, my children will not know how to sculpt unless they learn as well. They cannot inherit something that I learned without learning it themselves. The same is true of animals. They may learn something during their lifetime that is unique. For instance, I saw a wren use a piece of straw to coax a grub from a hole in a tree. It actually learned how to use a tool. Its offspring probably learned the trick as well from observing the parent. But if they did not observe it, they did not mystically have the ability because Mom or Dad had it.

When I opt not to walk down a dark alley, it is not because my instinct has kicked in, it is because I have seen enough television to know, or at least imagine, that bad things happen in dark alleys. My experience and common sense kicks in. How could that be instinctive when there were no alleys to walk down for my early ancestors? They were country folk. Similarly, when a deer emerges from the protective woods to an open meadow ripe with sweet summer grass, it is not instinct, but experience and heightened senses that engage and tell it to exercise caution. The deer has learned that stepping from the cover of the trees and undergrowth exposes it to the eyes of predators and hunters, and it must exercise due caution.

If you were to take an adult deer that had been the family pet all of its life and place it in the wild with predators, it would not last long because it has no experience. It has never seen a predator or hunter or has a reason to find settings that provide cover. Due to its familiarity with humans, it might even walk right up to a hunter, instead of fleeing. It knows nothing of that type of danger. It may be apprehensive of the new environment as any of us would be, but it will stroll without caution to its doom and no instinct will come to its rescue.

Clearly, however, what animals do have is an early warning system. Depending on the type of animal, one or more of their five senses are usually much more acute than ours. A dog has smell capability many thousands of times greater than ours. Some birds can see from the distance of a mile what you and I can only see from just a few feet. I have found that most mammals can feel percussions, such as explosions and earthquakes, many seconds before we feel them.

When a horse on a northern California ranch begins to act funny, perks up his ears, and displays apparent agitation moments before a large tremor is felt or before a fire line is seen on the horizon in the forest, does this mean the horse *knows* it is going to happen? The answer is no. It means that his five finely tuned senses allowed him to feel the vibration, smell the smoke, or interpret any other indicators long before our inferior senses were able to.

I do not have to prove any of these contentions. These are items of common knowledge. Animals usually have far superior senses than humans. Usually, the only time our senses become acute or superior to other human beings is after another of our senses is significantly dulled or even lost. For instance, a blind person, losing the ability to see, usually develops a keener sense of hearing, smell, and touch. I have a hearing loss in the high-frequency range. My low-frequency hearing is much keener now than it used to be, presumably to compensate for the loss of high frequency. In my case, I cannot say it is an advantage though. While I now am not bothered by the high-pitch noise of summer crickets that plague my wife, I can hear boom mobiles (cars with loud music) coming from six blocks away instead of the normal two.

From some of the correspondence I receive from readers, it has become clear to me that many believe me to be a man of small stature and retiring demeanor. I suppose some people jump to that conclusion because I have a gentle heart and am a student of the Bible. To many, to be a student of the Bible means you are not a strong individual. Somehow, they think the words "meek" and "weak" mean the same thing.

The fact is, I am over six feet tall, hold a second-degree black belt in Shotokan karate, am as solid as a rock, and possess a very outgoing personality. I am most comfortable in the desert, woods, swamp, or seashore, close to nature. I prefer the Everglades. I have removed alligators and rattlesnakes from the yards of people in distress, have wrestled a bear (okay, it was the Coast Guard Academy's mascot, weighed only 100 pounds, and I lost—so what), and have been bitten or stung by just about everything and anything that crawls on God's green earth or white sand.

I am a nature person. If I do not come home from a day of leisure in nature smelling like the swamp I played in, sporting several stings and bites, I probably did not have a good time. I say all that to qualify myself as someone who knows animals, domestic and wild, not some lethargic author who sits and stagnates all day long, expecting you to accept what I say simply because it is what I think.

Having said what I have said about animals not having a sixth sense, let me say now that this chapter really is not about animals. It is about people. More specifically, it is about the sixth sense that people possess. I want to discuss the theory of animals having a sixth sense in order to distinguish the difference between their perceived supernatural abilities and the real supernatural abilities of everyday people. Before anyone gets the wrong idea, let me quickly say that I am not speaking of what has come to be known as the "paranormal." I am not talking about mediums or palm readers. I am not talking about people who claim to be telekinetic or have ESP. I am not speaking of those people who society singles out and falsely labels supernaturally gifted. The people I speak of are everyday people and include every single person who has or ever will walk this earth.

Much of what I write about comes from experience and things I have learned from someone else along life's way. However, this one thing that I want to share with you comes from my own heart and perception of life. I have never heard this from anyone else or have I read it in anyone else's writings, so I take full blame for any issue you take with me over it. That notwithstanding, I am overjoyed to share it with you as my own idea, because few true original thoughts ever come to a person. Usually, when I happen upon what I consider a unique and profound thought, my glee is short lived because I soon realize someone else already thought of it. There was a period in my life when I dabbled in inventing. It seemed that whenever I conceived of a product that would prove useful, within days I would see a television commercial advertising a similar product. There are just too few original thoughts.

In fact, in the Old Testament book of Ecclesiastes, King Solomon asked, *"Is there any new thing under the sun?"* If you read that book, especially the first chapter, you will realize as Solomon did that there are very few new things that occur under the sun (or in this life). Most, if not all, have occurred before. Someone either did it before or said it before or conceived it before. That is just the way life is. It is hard to have a creative thought with six-billion other minds working at the same time.

So while my idea may not be very profound, it is nevertheless unique, and I hope it helps you understand some things about yourself.

I must begin by giving you some background information about myself. I know sometimes I take the long way of getting to a point, but sometimes that allows for a better understanding of the point being made. It certainly helps me explain things in a way that even I can understand. Besides, I think this background will facilitate your understanding of the concept I am going to share if you see how it worked in my own life first. It will not take long, and I believe you will find it interesting.

If you haven't already discovered this, I want you to know that I believe the Bible. I don't just believe in it or believe it's a good book. I don't just believe that it contains the Word of God. I believe it entirely and without reservation. I believe everything it says. That was not always true. In fact, I used to look upon the Bible with much doubt and suspicion. I thought it was like every other book, written by men who could and probably did make mistakes, men who were subject to personal bias and prejudice. Through a series of events, I came to learn that the Bible was in fact written by men, but they were men who were supernaturally inspired to write what they were directed to write. They'd no choice but to write what they were instructed to write. What a difference that made in the way I viewed this blessed book.

Since that revelation, I have studied in depth the inspiration and preservation of the Word of God and can say without reservation that this book is unlike any other. It is alive. It is supernatural. It is authoritative. It is the transmitted and recorded mind of the true, living God. If someone does not believe that, he or she might as well close it and set it on a shelf. If you do not believe the Bible to be the Word of the living God, it can do you no good. If you cannot believe the whole, how can you trust any part?

Briefly, I want to explain how this change came upon me. In 1974, I was a karate instructor in Hawaii. I was in the United States Navy by day and a karate instructor by night. I was on the go eighty hours a week and shamefully had very little time for my wife and children. My wife and I talked about my schedule, and we were both concerned that we were drifting apart and that our kids would have to endure a broken marriage. As semi-religious people, we both worried about that. We also worried that this could cause our children to turn away from God. This bothered me a lot, but I was in a tough spot. I loved my wife and kids, but I loved my fighting too. Karate was the joy in my life then. I had excelled at this art and won an open Hawaii Championship. I had over one thousand students and was somebody in one of the largest organizations of karate in the world.

Having been the proverbial "wimp" who was beaten up regularly by the tough kids at school all my life, I found being a fighting champion sat very well with me. Still, I knew something was missing in my family life. So in my own way, although not yet a Christian, I asked God to help me teach my children about him. Little did I suspect that it would be me who received the lesson.

Not long after that, I was teaching one of my many karate classes at an elementary school one evening in Waipahu on the island of Oahu. I'd given my class a break and I was taking one myself. I stood outside enjoying the Hawaiian moonlight and sweet smell of the plumeria flowers. After a few moments, I heard singing coming across the ball field from a church about two hundred yards away. They were singing a song called "Victory in Jesus" (I learned the title later). I had been to many churches and heard a lot of singing, but I'd never heard anything like this before. There was something very special about this church. These people sang as if they meant the words. They didn't have the best voices, but their song wasn't mechanical or meaningless like so many I'd heard at other times. From across the field I could feel great joy in their voices. The words they were singing obviously meant something very personal to them.

The song ended as did the break I was giving my class, but the story does not. The very next day at work, a young man who worked for me, approached me, wanting to speak to me. He wanted to speak about spiritual things. This was not unusual for him as he had done this with others in the office. It was just unusual that he should be speaking to me since I was his supervisor and in those days quite an intimidating sort.

While speaking with him, I discovered that he attended the church where I had heard the singing the night before. It seemed like a very strange coincidence to me, but I knew the young man did not know that I taught at the school next door to his church or that I had overheard the music. I had not told anyone, not even my class. I had just privately enjoyed it, filed it away in my memory, and then gone about my business. There is absolutely no way he could have known. Many months later we spoke of this situation, and he confirmed that he had not been aware of those things. It was clear to me that God was working behind the scenes as I had asked him to just days earlier.

Over the several weeks that followed, this young man continued to speak to me about the Bible and the Lord. I would protest about the Bible he was quoting, but he would respond with "But the Bible says . . ." and then he would give me another verse. It was quite frustrating. I quickly grew very weary of his steadfastness and eventually told him that I wanted nothing more to do with him. In fact (and please do not laugh at my immaturity), one day I grew so frustrated with him that I picked him up and actually hung him on a clothes hook in the back room of our office and left him hanging there. Others eventually helped him down.

He had every right to be angry with me, but if he was, he did not show it. Instead, he displayed great restraint and continued to speak with me whenever I gave him the opportunity. God was faithful and kept that young man after me. One day he pushed the envelope too far again saying once too many times "But the Bible says . . ." and I had to stop him. I just could not agree with him, and I could not let his persistent insinuation that the Bible was the authority on everything go by the boards. I stopped him and said in a rather loud voice and sarcastic tone, "Stop it— everyone knows the Bible is full of contradictions."

I was so proud of myself. My words seemed so profound and authoritative. To my amazement, however, this did not seem to rattle him. Instead, it appeared I had said exactly what he wanted me to say. He quickly and deliberately responded by asking, "How do you know that, Gary?" Now I was the one who was rattled. That question hit me hard. How indeed did I know that? I had never read the Bible. It was just my opinion, and I wondered where I had gotten that opinion from. Being an honest man, I tried to give him a truthful answer. I did not really want to say what I said; I knew I was giving him back the momentum in the conversation, but I responded, "I don't really know, Larry."

I never told him, but in those few moments before I responded, inside I was busily tossing around a lot of thoughts, such as Wow, why do I think the Bible has errors? Who made me think that? Maybe it isn't. And if it isn't, if the Bible is true, then there is a God, and that means there is a devil too, because God says there is—and if I am confused about God, and if I have trouble believing his word, I don't think it would be God confusing me—then it must be the devil.

And those thoughts scared me. I felt woozy. The room was swaying. Something was beginning to stir inside of me. There was a realization that maybe God was real after all. Oh, I know most of us believe God exists, but this was different—this was personal—God became personally real to me. It was difficult to think clearly with all these thoughts flooding my mind. On top of that, I could see Larry beaming, not in a gloating way, but as if he had just helped a blind person to cross the street. His look of triumph was not offensive but more of an invitation to seek more help. And I decided I needed more help. I needed answers fast and I started asking questions in earnest.

A few days later after my friend had answered all my questions and showed me what the Bible had to say about this and that, the authority of God's Word hit me like a ton of bricks, or at least what I imagined a ton of bricks would feel like if I were to be hit by them. It all started to fit together in my mind and make sense. Whatever was stirred inside of me a few days earlier was now fully awakened. I came to realize that I was lost and without hope, even though I considered myself a good person, a religious person. I was friendly, warm, and compassionate. I did good things and treated people respectfully. I thought I was the kind of person God would find favor with, even the kind of person he would want on his side. Isn't that how we all feel about ourselves?

I saw in God's Word though that I was not "good" in the Bible sense of the word—that no one is. His Word says, "There is none righteous, no not one," "For all have sinned and come short of the glory of God," and "All your righteousness [goodness] is as filthy rags." That was hard to accept, that God considered my good no better than filthy rags. I learned later that the indication was that if I came to him in my own perceived righteousness, instead of being clothed in his pure righteousness, my spiritual garment would appear as filthy rags to him and fall far short. It was clear to me that I needed God's goodness and not my own.

It was as if God had flipped a spotlight on me and opened up my understanding. My soul was in great turmoil and unrest. I had this tremendous "truth" revealed to me and did not know what to do with it. My mind was racing as quickly as my heart. For the first time in my life, I realized that the Bible was true. I realized that God stepped into my life as I had asked him to. I realized that all my religion and all my own goodness had afforded me nothing. I was still not right with God. Eventually, and I might say also inevitably, I found myself on my knees in my bathroom weeping and asking God to forgive me. I told him I was sorry for all I had ever done wrong and that I just wanted Jesus in my life.

You want to talk about miracles! In an instant I was changed—my whole life, my whole outlook, my whole attitude, my whole direction in life. Without trying to sound humorous, my whole afterlife direction changed too, if you know what I mean. It was overwhelming.

Five minutes earlier I was in complete turmoil with the weight of the world and my sin on my shoulders. Moments later, I did not have a care in the world, and the best thing was I knew I had been born again by the Spirit of God through the shed blood of Jesus Christ. I am not a person who is easily influenced. I am one of those analytical people who want to look at something, evaluate it, look again, question it, and shake it for a while to see what might come out of it, before deciding if I want to accept it. But here was spiritual evidence to the truth I had been told. In an instant my heart felt like it was new. Now I am not talking about the literal pumping organ in my chest. I mean rather my mind, the seat of my consciousness, where God does business with us. One moment you are in darkness, and the next you see everything with blinding-light understanding and with a clarity that can only come from the Father. One moment I was worried about dying, about money, about cancer, about nuclear war, about my future, and about the future of my family, and the next moment, every burden was lifted from my heart and I was set free. Immediately, I knew there had been a change. I now belonged to the Lord, and I knew for the first time in my life with certainty that he existed and that he was in charge.

It has taken me some time to get to the point that I want to make, but I am finally here. I hope my personal story has not offended you. I feel it is the best illustration I can offer for the point I want to make next. Focus with me if you will on that very moment I determined I wanted my children to know about God. That was no accident. Something inside me moved me to be concerned. At some time in our lives, usually when we are younger, but not always, we all wonder or suspect that there is a greater power in control. In the book of Romans, we are told that humankind knows that God exists in one of three ways: by our conscience, by the intricacies of nature around us verifying a master design or plan, or by the Word of God, which clearly discloses this fact.

The proof for this assertion can be seen around the world—actually through my service in the United States Navy for the first eight years of my military career and vicariously through the many missionaries I have met, I have been exposed to the cultures of many nations around the globe. Based on my experiences, I can tell you that if you were to visit other cultures in our world today, you would find many religious practices and values much different from our own.

Some cultures would appall your sense of dignity and morality. You might even consider some so pagan as to be beyond being civilized. If you look closely at each culture, however, you will find evidence of deity awareness. If you were to go to the darkest jungles, where even to this day civilization has not transgressed, you would possibly find natives bowing down to the head of a pig impaled on top of a spear or worshiping an idol fashioned from raw materials from the forest.

It seems no matter how deeply you travel into the bush, how far back in time we might go (figuratively speaking of backward cultures), or how godless the people appear to be, you will always find some form of deity worship, some form of religion. Awareness of God is universal. As I considered this, as I studied the word of God, and as I recalled the literally thousands of conversations I have had with people about God, a thought occurred to me. And that thought was this: that all people everywhere, in every time and in every culture, have something within them that tells them there is a God.

They do not acquire this sense; it is just there within them. They may stray from the innocence of this realization later in their lives, depending on their denominational affiliation and personal experiences, but that sense that there is a God is inside all of us from the start. This sense is not optional equipment, but standard factory issue. It knows no race or gender. It is within each heart, placed there by the creator, God. It reflects the just eye of God, in that he sees no race or gender, and it ensures that all men and all women are equally made with regard to their awareness of God's existence and their having the opportunity to accept him.

It does not matter if you are born into royalty or to a poor gaucho on a South American ranch. It does not matter if you are the child of a minister or if your parents are professed atheists. It is in you. It is a true *sixth sense* if you will—not sight, not hearing, not taste, not smell, and not touch, but something more. It is not something that heightens the other senses, as is the case with animals, for we are made differently from the animals, in God's image. This true sixth sense is something higher and universal, something that elevates our attention beyond the realm of our earthly existence. It gives us an awareness that something more and beyond our physical existence is there.

I have labeled this sixth sense SONG, or Sense of Our Need for God. Whether or not we are willing to admit it, inside each of us there exists an emptiness, one that cannot be filled or satisfied by temporal or earthly things. We may have a successful and satisfying life. We may have amassed great wealth or achieved most or all the goals we have set for ourselves. We may have attained fame or made a lasting contribution to society that gives us great personal satisfaction. Still, if we do not have a personal relationship with God, we have an empty void within us.

As an adult, you may not agree. Perhaps you have resisted, even ignored that empty feeling. Maybe you have turned from God. Maybe you are an agnostic, or maybe you are an atheist who has what you consider an ironclad case to prove God does not exist. But I would wager you were not always so. I would imagine that as a child, you had the innocence that every child possesses, and there was a time when God was real to you.

I have ministered to hundreds of children in my lifetime, and I have never met a child who could not believe in God. Children are inquisitive and ask many questions about God, but I have never had one tell me he or she did not believe in him. There has not been time enough in their young lives for the world to harden their tender hearts or to fill their innocent minds with religious error or humanism.

Mark, in his gospel, records the very words of Jesus confirming this. In chapter 10, verse 14, the Lord says:

*Suffer the little children to come unto me, and
forbid them not: for of such is the kingdom of God.*

Jesus was addressing the innocence of children, but he was applying that innocence as the criteria for anyone who would enter his kingdom. To enter his kingdom or, in other words, to have a personal relationship with him, a person must display childlike trust in him and him alone. My experience has been that children do not feel the spiritual emptiness that adults feel. Perhaps it would be more accurate for me to say that adults no longer feel the innocence that they felt as children. Innocence accepts that there is a God. Lack of innocence creates a void within. And in his omniscience, God placed within each heart that SONG so that when we feel that emptiness, we might recognize our need for him and long after him.

I am sure that I will receive correspondence from so-called Bible scholars to argue that point. Before you write, however, consider this question. What is the Bible? Is it merely a collection of poetic and historical books that were written by men to bring moral and ethical order to our world? Or is it what it claims to be: the preserved and perfect Word of God, a projection of his mind and will—a collection of poetry, songs, and rules for life, service, and salvation. I believe it is the latter and that the sum of God's Word can be compacted into one statement. The Word of God is God's love letter to his creation and the revelation of his son, the Lord Jesus Christ, as the savior of the world.

If we believe that God loves us (and he most certainly does), then we can conclude that he wants us to love him in return. In Matthew 22:37, Jesus was asked what the greatest of all the commandments was. His response was:

That you love the Lord thy God with all thy heart,
with all thy soul, and with all thy mind.

When we love someone, is it not our foremost desire that he or she love us back? If we could, would we not put something in that person's heart that would cause them to long for us as we long for them? Let us set aside for a moment the strong support that we have in the Word of God for this position and just apply our reason and logic. Would it not be reasonable to believe that God, with his perfect love and longing for us, would want to put something in our hearts that would cause us to long for him? Of course, it would!

While the label I have placed on this sixth sense, SONG, is a product of my own creativity, the concept is well established in God's Word. There can be no doubt but that scripture inspired my creativity and all the credit belongs to God. Indeed, every time I read the powerful Word of God, it educates me and provokes me to meditate and think. It draws me closer to God. Psalm 40, one of the many psalms written by David, the King of Israel, is a good example of this. Verse 3 had a profound effect on me. It reads:

And he hath put a new song in my mouth, even praise unto our God.

As I read this, I wondered, If David is speaking of a new song, then there must be an old song. What was the old song? One could suppose that he was speaking strictly of music, but I do not think that is so. All the psalms are in and of themselves songs, hymns, or prayers sung by the Jews. However, each psalm has spiritual meaning and application too, not only to the Jew, but to New Testament Christians as well.

My curiosity was heightened. What was David's old song? Please note that I had already come up with my acronym of SONG. I just happened upon this psalm later and it prompted me to examine David's thoughts in conjunction with my own. I then did what is normal for me in my study of the Word—I looked back a bit before Psalm 40 to see what David might have been referring to. In the Thirty-ninth Psalm, I found something that caught my attention. For sake of space I will not reproduce the entire psalm here, but the essence of David's thoughts seem to be that he was contemplating eternity (see especially verse 4).

Now, for you Bible students, I am well aware that David was dealing with other issues at this time in his life. I am not trying to lessen the importance of that. I am merely trying to show that David was like most people, we all think about the frailness of our existence and wonder what lies at the end of our road. When we think of these things, invariably one thought, one name, comes to mind—God. That thought is in all of us from the start. We may subdue it or bury it as we age. We might even kill the awareness altogether through sinful and wild living, but we begin life with it fully intact, every one of us throughout the history of humankind.

It may seem a bit of a stretch to you, but I believe that David's old song was this awareness speaking inside of him. He was concerned about eternity and God. What better sense could we ask for but to have something within us that tells us that God exists? People have lived without sight. They have lived without touch and without the ability to hear or smell or taste. For whatever reasons, God sometimes allows deficiencies in these natural senses, but God has never allowed anyone to be born void of SONG.

In anticipation that some might ask, but what of those who are born with diminished mental capacities? let me briefly address that without wandering too far from our study. The Bible teaches that every human being who is of the age of understanding must be born again to have a right relationship with God. In other words, when a child is old enough to know the difference between right and wrong and chooses to do wrong, that child has reached the age of understanding. As well that child is accountable for his or her own actions.

Obviously, this age is different for all children, but my opinion is that this always occurs before a child becomes a teenager. So then, children who have reached this age of accountability must be born again or "saved" by repenting of his or her personal sins and placing his or her trust in the Lord Jesus Christ.

Before this age occurs, if children prematurely pass away, they are not saved, but are rather "safe" in the Lord. In other words, since they have not reached the age where they would be held accountable for their own actions, the Lord has made provision for them. They are safe and in no danger of missing heaven.

In keeping with God's provision, we can apply the logic that God has endowed us to speak to the issue of the mentally diminished. In effect, those who do not have the mental capacity to understand their responsibility of repentance and faith, remain children or childlike in their understanding, irrespective of their age. They do not have discernment, and they are not held accountable. They, too, are safe, so do not let that weigh on your mind. God has a contingency for all situations.

Even someone not acquainted at all with the Bible knows the famous phrase "All men are created equal." Is this true? If it is, then why can't I dunk the ball like Michael Jordan? If it's true, why can't I sing like Elvis? Why are some unfortunate people born with mental and physical defects? Why are some born in oppressed countries and afforded less freedom than my dog? The fact is we aren't all born physically or geographically equal. We're born spiritual equals. We are all equally endowed with that SONG. Created in his image, God has graciously placed that sense of our need for him within each of us.

God also provides a response to our SONG. His love is extended to each of us through his son, the Lord Jesus Christ. And Jesus is revealed to us by the Word of God. He has commissioned many, like some of you and me, to bring that Word to every corner of the globe. He has ensured that every person, every nation, and every era in history has had access to the knowledge of his Son. Even before the birth of Jesus, the Old Testament pointed forward to him as the Messiah. The Roman governor knew of him before his birth, for he sent messengers to tell him when the birth of the Messiah took place in Bethlehem.

Every human being who comes forth from the womb has this sense of a need for God. I believe it fuels our conscience and trips our sense of good and evil. As I said earlier, some, through the lifestyles they choose or through the erroneous influence of others, lose touch with the sense that there is a God and that they need him. However, this does not change that need that they have for him.

Everyone who is born is born away from God and must reconcile with him in this lifetime. Fortunately, we do not have to appease him ascetically. We do not have to pilgrimage on our knees for hundreds of miles to satisfy his wrath. We do not have to pay money to find forgiveness. Oh no, for that forgiveness has already been purchased by the precious blood of his own Son. All we have to do is accept the work God has already done to effect that reconciliation. All we have to do is follow God's simple plan.

Briefly, we need to hear the truth. We then need to make a mental ascent to that truth that it is true. And finally, we have to make an appropriation of that truth to ourselves. I have given you the truth in this chapter. We all are sinners in need of reconciliation with God (see Roman 3:10 and 3:23). God has provided the means, the only means for that reconciliation (see John 3:16). You need to determine in your heart that what God's Word tells you is true, that you are in need, and that he has supplied the way for you. Finally, the most important step, you need to make it personal. Jesus did not just die for the whole world, he died for you. You need to invite him into your heart and let his atonement apply to you.

If you have heard the truth (and you have), if you believe the truth (and I hope you do), and if you want to make that personal appropriation, it is a very simple matter to take care of. The following is a sample prayer, something similar to what I prayed when I asked Jesus into my heart, very similar also to what people pray when they ask him to save them. It is only a sample. You can pray using any similar wording you desire, it really does not matter. The only thing that matters is that you are sincere. You must believe what you are praying. I cannot do that for you.

Sample Prayer

*Father, I understand that I am a sinner and that
Jesus died on the cross for me, in my place. I am
sorry for my sin. I ask your forgiveness. I want
to have a new relationship with you and invite Jesus
into my heart.*

Is that not simple? I have met people who have told me that
no, it can't be that easy—it is too simple. And indeed, it really is
simple. It is just a matter of faith—accepting the good news that
God has revealed to us in his word through his son. The good
news is that we were lost and God has found us. The good news
is that we were sinners, but Christ paid the price for our sins.
The good news is that we had no hope, but now in Christ we all
have hope. But along with the good news, comes some very bad
news.

In Proverbs 14:12 we are told:

*There is a way that seemeth right unto a man, but
the end thereof are the ways of death.*

God apparently thinks this message is so important that just
two chapters later, in Proverbs 16:25, he repeats that warning
again, word for word. God knows us better than we know ourselves. He knows that we are prone to be religious, but not necessarily religiously right.

As simple to understand as the gospel of Jesus Christ is, there
are so many who would complicate it and make it difficult. They

will add something to it, such as baptism, or take something away, such as repentance, thereby confusing those they influence. That is why God warns us to be sure to follow his way and not the way of men. You will find no shortage of the ways of men, but there is only one God way.

The bad news is that once you hear the good news you have to make a decision, and too often people make the wrong one and decide that they are okay. They have been a member of this church or that church forever and surely their minister knows what is right. Or maybe Mom and Dad used to go here, or maybe Grandpa is buried in the churchyard. For the sake of tradition, without checking it out for themselves in the Word that God has written, they decide to follow the way they think is right. And that truly is bad news.

Let me close with a story that will help illustrate what I am trying to get across to you. In the earlier part of the last century, a local train was delivering schoolchildren home from school one afternoon. As the slow-moving train rounded a bend, it developed engine problems and came to a stop. The engineer, realizing that a fast-moving commuter train would be coming on the same track about ten or fifteen minutes later, ordered his assistant to run back beyond the bend and signal the train to stop. The man ran with all of his might and got to the flag signal station just as the commuter train was coming into view.

The man grabbed the red flags from the station, stepped out on the track, and waved the flags vigorously high over his head. To his horror, the commuter train did not slow down. He waved more frantically until the train was almost on top of him, and then he jumped off the track. The engineer of the second train waved as he went by without even slowing. As the flagman watched the second train disappear around the bend, he heard the sound of screeching metal upon metal and the inevitable percussion of a great collision. There was much carnage in this great tragedy.

In the months following, an investigation was conducted to determine what had happened. The magistrate first questioned the flagman. "Sir, your job was to signal the approaching commuter train. Did you do your job?"

"Yes, sir," he said. "I waved the red flags high over my head vigorously."

"And what was the result?" the magistrate asked.

"To my surprise and horror, the engineer of the train did not even slow down. He merely waved at me and continued on his way," the flagman answered.

The magistrate dismissed the flagman and called for the engineer of the commuter train to take the stand. "Sir, you have heard the testimony that you were flagged down. How is it that you failed to stop?" the magistrate asked.

The engineer responded, "Your honor, indeed this man was on the tracks waving the flags as he has testified. But the flags were not red as he supposed, but were yellow. To an engineer, the yellow flag means that I may continue on without reducing speed, but to be alert for changes. It was only after I came around the bend that I was aware of the school train, and I tried with all my earthly might to bring my train to a halt. I sincerely regret that I was not able to do so."

At an apparent impasse, the magistrate sent for the flags from the very station in question. Upon arrival, the flags were inspected. It was found that indeed they had once been red, but because of exposure to the rain and other elements, they had faded to a dull yellow. The tragedy was the result of the wrong message being sent. A red flag of warning was needed, but a flag of caution was waved instead.

I submit to you that all over this world there are men and women who are preaching a yellow gospel. They are waving the wrong flags. When they should be waving flags of warning, they are only suggesting caution and sending people to spiritual tragedy. To them the good news is living a good life. And there is nothing wrong with living a good life. But that is not the gospel of Jesus Christ. To them the good news is doing good things for other people. And there is nothing wrong with doing good things. But it is not the gospel of Jesus Christ.

If this chapter offends you, I extend my sincerest apologies; that was not my intention. I simply will not wave a yellow flag at you. The gospel of Jesus Christ is that we were in need of a savior and God sent his Son, Jesus, to be that savior. There is no other way to get to God's heaven than to trust the Lord Jesus as your own savior. My hope and desire is that you have already trusted him. If you have not, then my prayer is that you will.

Chapter 10

CAN THE SPIRITS OF ANIMALS RETURN TO EARTH?

This is one topic that evokes more interest from people than you might expect. You may have wondered about this yourself. Almost daily I receive a letter or e-mail from someone wanting to know if it is possible that his or her pet's spirit has returned to visit the family. In fact, I have received so much mail on this topic that it became prudent for me to find a place to discuss it in this book.

When people who love animals lose a cherished best friend, it is often one of (if not) the most traumatic experiences of their life. If the grief and pain were not enough, they are suddenly asking themselves questions they would never have guessed they would ask one day: Is there an animal afterlife? Do animals have souls? Is there some way that I can contact them? Not having the answers themselves, they turn outward looking for someone, or anyone who can give them insight or comfort. In this state of mind, they are very vulnerable to those who would take advantage of or exploit their need. Unfortunately, they will find no shortage of New Age writings that will provide answers without base or substance. They say what their authors perceive people want to hear to make sales, but what they say is so outrageous that people wind up even more confused and unsure.

When profit is the motivator, content should be suspect. It is easy to write. Anyone can do it. But it takes passion and character to write something of substance that the reader can depend on as being valid and validated. Good writing should not be measured so much by grammar and punctuation as it is by the basis and justification for the thing being said.

Now to be fair, some useful contemporary writings (books, articles, website content, etc.) are available that appear to want genuinely to help readers. Still, without an authoritative basis like the Bible to give their thoughts credence, they come up lacking. Because someone can think a thing does not mean that thing is true. There must be a source of tried-and-tested truth to draw conclusions from. People who are burdened to their core with questions of passion like those mentioned previously want dependable answers and guidance. They have genuine concerns about what happens to their pets after they pass. To some these concerns may seem frivolous and silly, but to those of us who love our animals, we know how important qualitative answers to these questions and concerns are.

Usually, when I am asked if a pet can come back from beyond the grave, people are not merely being inquisitive. They have had some sort of bizarre or supernatural experience and wanted to share it with me to get my take on it. Invariably, what they are actually looking for is validation that it was their best friend trying to contact them. I do not summarily dismiss these inquiries as you might suppose. That is not what I do. Being dismissive serves no purpose. Though I am reluctant to label what I do "ministry," my calling, my responsibility is to help people find the biblical answers to their questions. More importantly, I am here to help people. I take my responsibilities seriously. To that end, I provide my personal e-mail address in all my books and articles and respond to every inquiry personally and, if I might add, quickly.

Furthermore, there are just too many instances, too many reports of this sort of experience to dismiss. In a short three-year period during which I kept track of the types of questions I was asked, more than 1,500 people asked postdeath-experience types of questions. It was clear to me that this was a topic in need of some solid biblical answers.

Before I accumulated those statistics and came to that realization, however, I admit that I would have my doubts when people contacted me. I still responded with kindness and answered their questions the best I could, but a little voice inside of me told me that their experiences were just wishful thinking, a reaction to the intense grief they were enduring.

The voice was wrong. It did not take the entire three years for me to know that something strange, perhaps even supernatural, was going on with some people who lost their pets. From tabloids to mainstream newspapers and periodicals, stories abound in human-interest sections that talk about pets coming back from the dead. There is account after account of sightings or apparitions or both. What is going on? Are departed pets indeed now angels as some New Age writers claim? Can pets really come back? And if they do not come back physically, can they come to us in our dreams? Can we trust that our dreams are some sort of sign, or is it just the pepperoni pizza we had for dinner kicking in?

Let me take time here to share some actual accounts given to me by readers for the benefit of those readers who have not had such an experience. I have permission from each reader to use his or her story, but most have asked to remain anonymous because they do not want their friends or family to think they have lost their minds. In fact, I have taken it an additional step by using fictitious people and pet names in place of the actual ones. So if you are one who has shared his or her story with me, any similarity you may see in your particular case will be purely coincidental.

I used no specific criteria in the selection of these stories other than I thought they provided a good representation of the types of e-mails and letters I had received. If you submitted a story to me and it was not included in this chapter, please know that it was only because another similar story was already selected. You will no doubt be looking for a solution to each story as you read it, but there will be none given. I have decided to address the individual cases collectively later on in the book and provide my own insight. I think you will understand why when we arrive at that point.

In no particular order of importance or significance, here are several accounts:

ROSCOE'S BELL

Nora contacted me in 1999 while I was living in Houston. She had lost her tabby Roscoe completely unexpectedly. Roscoe was a total house cat, neutered, declawed, and disinterested in ever going outdoors. Like all pets, Roscoe had a unique personality and way about him. He was the joy of Nora's life. He was smart too. Nora had jokingly placed a hotel bell on the counter, one of those contraptions they use to call bellboys with, and taught him to ring it. He did not ring it when he wanted to eat or anything like that, but every so often when he was on the counter, he would play with the bell and ring it repeatedly until he tired of it. When Nora was busy around the house, it served as a reminder of her love for Roscoe.

One morning the kitchen door was left open while a plumber moved in a new toilet and moved out the old. Roscoe was his typical nosey self and sniffed around the plumber's toolbox out of curiosity (and no this is not a curiosity killed the cat story). The toolbox was very close to the open door, and when the plumber dropped a tool with a loud bang, Roscoe jumped and landed on the other side of the threshold. He immediately crouched down in fear of this strange new environment.

Nora, seeing the danger, called as soothingly as she could and moved quickly toward him. Unfortunately, Roscoe panicked and ran off into the nearby bushes. Nora, in tears and with an apologetic plumber following close behind, quickly started searching and calling Roscoe's name. After many hours of searching, it was clear that Roscoe had run back deeper into the woods, and if he were to come home, he would have to find his own way back. Brokenhearted, Nora gave up the search and returned home.

When two months had passed, Nora completely gave up hope that Roscoe would ever return home. Indeed, because of the large coyote population in the area, she had resigned herself after just a couple of weeks that he had probably met with a very tragic fate. Early in the morning hours as she lay in bed, she heard the bell in the kitchen. As she was half-awake and half-asleep, she assumed that she had dreamed hearing the bell. But then, moments later it dinged again and then again.

Nora jumped up from bed and hurried into the kitchen, knocking over a chair and the trash pail on the way. She reached the light and flipped it on in great expectation. But there was no Roscoe. There was nobody. But she knew she had heard the bell. Picking it up, she examined it as if there were a clue to the mystery to be discovered. There was not. Several times after that experience, Nora heard the bell again. Each time she rushed into the kitchen, knocking over either the trash or the chair or both, only to find nothing. In anticipation of this phenomenon continuing, Nora wisely moved the trash and chair. Unfortunately, the bell never rang again.

Nora wrote to me to ask if it were possible that Roscoe would try to contact her. Had she missed the message? Was there something she could do? Nora assured me that she and Roscoe had lived alone. There were no other pets or people in the house. There was no other explanation for this bell ringing. It had been Roscoe's bell and she knew he was trying to contact her.

VANISHING BUSTER

Bob, an elderly gentleman, contacted me in almost complete distress. He did not write an e-mail or send a letter. Somehow, he found my telephone number and called me directly. I do not encourage people to call me, but I am gracious and responsive when they do. It just seems that when people do telephone, they often do not consider time differences. On those rare occasions when they do, they somehow add hours when they should subtract and vice versa. Seldom are their calculations in my favor. This time was no different. Bob called me at 3 A.M. in the morning. Fortunately, I think sleep is overrated, and I am happy to give it up when I am needed. I wake up and become alert very quickly. It did not take me long to catch on to what Bob was telling me. It was clear he was upset.

He and his wife had been grieving the loss of their Jack Russell terrier, Buster, for nearly six months. Their children and grandchildren lived far away, and Buster had been the joy of their lives for over fourteen years. Nothing tragic had happened to Buster. He just got old and it was his time to go on ahead. The fact that his passing was not due to an accident and not premature helped Bob and his wife cope, but somehow they just could not get over the loss. Almost nightly they knelt in prayer and asked God to make sure Buster was taken care of. Occasionally, emotions would take over and Bob would sob, "Lord please send him back, just for a little while." I think we have all been there.

One evening Bob, nearly asleep, but not quite there, sat up in bed. His wife asked, "What's wrong, dear?"

Bob said, "I don't know, I just feel something is not right." With that, he swung his legs over the edge of the bed and searched for his slippers. Suddenly, Bob saw in the dim light coming from the night-light in the bathroom down the hall, a silhouette in the doorway. It was the silhouette of a dog—of Buster! "Buster," Bob called out and ran to the doorway. "Buster, is that you?" The dog turned and ran down the hall into the guest bedroom. Bob was close enough behind to see the animal scurry under the bed. He rushed in, groping for the light switch. Finding it and switching the light on, with considerable physical difficulty, Bob knelt down and looked under the bed.

By this time Bob's wife had arrived and demanded to know what was going on. Bob briefly explained what he had seen and asked her to lift the bedspread on the opposite side of the bed so he might have more light to see. She complied, but there was no dog or any animal at all under the bed. Not even an old slipper or dust ball.

This was a one-time experience. It was never repeated. But Bob was sure of what he saw. He assured me that he had not been sleeping. He had been lying in bed thinking about some carpentry work that he had planned to do in the garage the next day. He did not hear any sound; he simply felt a presence in the room and jumped up in reaction to that. He assures me that it was not a dream. I believe him. I have lain awake calculating measurements and such myself. It is difficult to get sleepy when you have important things on your mind.

Bob wanted to know if he was going crazy. He asked if I thought this was really Buster or just his imagination working overtime. Bob was eager to invite him back again and wondered if God had sent him back as he had prayed and if God would do so again.

A CLOSE BRUSH

Mike contacted me after the loss of his wonderful cat, Ruby. He and Ruby had been very close. Ruby had contracted a terminal type of cancer, and all efforts to put it in remission had failed. Mike was forced to watch her wither away, but he spent all his spare time with her and talked to her. He begged her to come back or to give him a sign that she was okay after she passed. Mike finally let Ruby go, and it broke his heart as it does so many of us pet people. He spent his days trying to stay preoccupied with work and his nights sobbing along with his wife. It was tough, very tough. Grief allows us very little off time.

Just when Mike thought the pain could get no worse as he sat sobbing at his desk in the den, he felt something brush up against the back of his leg. It felt like a cat. It had to be Ruby! Startled and yet ecstatic, he looked down, but the sensation stopped and there was nothing there. Chuckling to himself about how one's mind can play such tricks, he turned back to his desk to try to pay some bills. Again the sensation came and this time there was no mistaking it. It was a cat rubbing on the back of his leg, his cat—Ruby. Again he looked down and again there was nothing there. Then the sensation was gone.

The experience was repeated a few more times that evening. One moment Mike thought he was going crazy and the next he knew he was not. Still, he opted not to mention the experience to his wife. Instead, he went on the web and searched to see if others had had similar experiences. He found many people who had such experiences but no answers to his questions. Eventually he found my website and addressed his questions to me.

UNMISTAKABLE

A teenage girl contacted me via e-mail (I made her have her mother telephone me with her approval before I communicated with her) with some real concerns about an experience she had. It seems she was dreaming about her dog Lasso, who had passed away several months earlier.

She explained that accepting Lasso's passing for her was not particularly difficult. She had wept a bit the first day, but her life was so full of things like school, friends, leisure time, and so on, that she just moved on rather quickly. But several months later she was dreaming about her dog, and the grief she felt in her dream was so overwhelming that she woke up sobbing almost uncontrollably. Through her sobs, she heard a distant bark coming from outside. The bark sounded very familiar and she felt the need to peek out of her window. There sitting in the yard, perhaps thirty yards from her window was Lasso. He was wagging his tail, looking directly at her, and letting out a couple of happy barks.

Though overwhelmed with emotion, she quickly ran from her room, down the hall, and out the kitchen door, which was the closest exit to where she had seen Lasso. She ran barefoot through the dew-soaked grass to the side of the house. When she turned the corner of the house to where she had seen Lasso, he was not there. She had the presence of mind to look at the spot where she had thought she saw Lasso. It was obvious that the dew had been disturbed. There were no paw prints leading to or away from the disturbed spot, but there was no mistake—something had been sitting there not too long ago.

Her experience was a one-time thing, but it left such an impression on her that she was determined to see if anyone else had had a similar experience. In her search, she came across many of the flippant writings I just mentioned before, and they served only to confuse and frustrate her. Finally, she came across my website and contacted me. I was able to help her. I offered a solid case of what the Bible has to say about this sort of phenomenon or anomaly. I explained that the Bible takes a strong stand against people seeking to contact those who have passed on and tells us that it is impossible for those who have passed to contact us, be they human or animal.

Again, I believe these few showcase experiences are a good representation of the types of inquiries I receive regarding this phenomenon of alleged "ghost pets," and they probably mirror the experiences some of you have had. There is definitely something going on; I have to admit that. There are just too many instances of things like this happening for us simply to label them imagination or dreams. Biblically eliminating the possibility that departed animals are able to visit or contact us does not necessarily deny that people are experiencing the things they report. It is quite easy to reconcile both ideas from a biblical standpoint. While former inhabitants of earth are unable to visit us, other beings are.

We are told in Ephesians 6:12 of our struggle in life:

For we wrestle not against flesh and blood, but against principalities, against powers, against the rulers of the darkness of this world, against spiritual wickedness in high places.

Those principalities and powers are deceiving some. For reasons I cite in the following chapters, the spiritual wickedness in this world has an agenda of deceit. They know no bounds in their rebellion against God and hate for humanity. I will delve into this in great detail ahead, and I assure you, you shall find great comfort in some of the things I will be sharing with you.

Chapter 11

UNDERSTANDING THE
PHENOMENON

In this and the following chapters, we are going to look at what the Bible has to say on this alleged phenomenon I like to term "ghost pets" or the claim that departed pets can and do return to this life to visit their people. My purpose is not to refute the erroneous views of nontraditional or New Age writers but rather to give a clear and concise Bible position. Readers can draw their own conclusions based on the evidence provided.

Perhaps more than any other topic, people seem to be most stubborn about the Bible, holding on vehemently to whatever concepts and beliefs they have been taught in their formative years. As in my personal case, it does not matter if they have had any experience or exposure to scripture; they simply know what they know and that is the sum of their argument. Christians learn early on that it seldom accomplishes anything to argue Bible. No true victory is achieved in winning the argument if in doing so you lose the person you are trying to enlighten. It is better just to quote the Bible and let it do what it promises to do, to touch

144

the heart of the hearer. Its authority and power will reprove error and send it reeling in retreat.

If you recall my confrontations with Larry in chapter 9, you know that I have firsthand experience with this principle. It was used against my argument quite successfully. Larry could never have convinced me, but the scripture he gave me was seeded into my soul, took root, and grew. In the end, it was the planted seed of scripture and not the words of Larry that won the day.

Because this topic is as difficult to present as it is important to know, I will be relying on direct quotes from scripture more than I do in other chapters to make my points. Some of my views may come across as "old hat." Admittedly, they are. While society may be progressive and always changing, the Bible is not. It, like God, is immutable. It never changes. You will find those who will change what it says to try to tickle the ears of readers, all for the sake of making a profit, but that will not be the case here. You will get the straight story and the whole story without ulterior motive.

This chapter is going to be a hard pill for some to swallow, especially for those who have been through an experience of being contacted by a deceased pet as just described. It is difficult for some to accept what the Bible says over the experience they have had, but the heart that wants to know the truth will seek it out. Accordingly, I ask that you please hear me out and then ask that you defer your reaction to what you read in this chapter until you have completed reading the following three chapters.

Chapters 11 14 are designed to be read together to give the reader the complete picture. Whatever feathers this chapter might ruffle, I assure you the following chapter will smooth them out again. At first glance, there may appear to be some contrast in what is being said, but in fact the thoughts mesh together perfectly in many ways to offer a very solid alternative explanation of the issues surrounding these alleged supernatural experiences.

So what about this phenomenon some are calling ghost pets? Are our pets indeed able to return to us physically or visit us in our dreams to comfort us? Are they trying to reach out to us or tell us something? Is God allowing this experience to help us in our grief? The quick answer to most of these questions might initially upset you because it is an unwavering no. But I know that this simple answer will not suffice. A more detailed and convincing answer is needed and will be provided in the following pages.

To prove my case and provide those answers, I will need to not only quote scripture, as I alluded to earlier, but also build on principles found in the Word of God. Admittedly, sometimes there are just no passages that say exactly what we hope they will say. For instance, no verse is available that specifically says that pets cannot return from the dead. To be fair, however, this is often the case in nondoctrinal issues. Often, no specific scripture can be found that one may cite, but somehow we know by the gist of what is said what is right or wrong on that particular issue. For instance, no verse admonishes me not to throw water balloons at the elderly, but I know from other principles taught in scripture concerning deportment and respect that this behavior is not acceptable. Applying the reasoning abilities that God gave to me, I can discern from a collective view of associated principles what my behavior toward the elderly (and all other persons for that matter) should be and can logically conclude that throwing water balloons is not acceptable.

The next step is to apply contextual criticism to a passage (who is talking, who are they talking to, why is the thing being said, what were the circumstances that caused it to be said, etc.). This is appropriate exegesis of scripture, or rightly dividing the word of truth. The Bible itself sanctions this sort of study ("Study to show thyself approved unto God . . . rightly dividing the word of truth"). Often nothing good comes from snatching a single verse out of scripture and building a doctrine around it. In fact, this technique is often the catalyst for religious error.

The fundamental principle in proper discernment is to ensure that your understanding lines up with other, associated scripture. If what you think is in contrast with another portion of scripture, then you are wrong. If what you think does not line up with all other scripture, but lines up with most of it, then you are still wrong. Your idea must line up with the rest of the Bible 100 percent of the time in order for it to be valid. God does not make mistakes. His thoughts are always constant and never contrast or confuse. The Bible says that God is not the author of confusion. I think you know who is.

Accordingly, where the scripture states a thing clearly, I will provide it verbatim. Where principle should be applied, I will carefully build upon what is being said and show the associated teachings to ensure that there is no contrast. Applying these strict criticisms will ensure that we can trust the principles that come into focus. Now then, it seems the first thing we would want to establish is whether animals can return to earth from the dead. You might suppose that would be not only the first thing we wanted to know but the only thing. It is not. Irrespective of what answer we find, there are going to be more questions. So let us call the issue of whether animals can return from the dead the first item for discussion.

We have already acknowledged that the Bible does not specifically address this issue in relation to animals. In this case, we would want to look for evidence that tells us whether God allows people to return to earth after death. This will give us a potential precedent. We have employed this principle before without prejudice, and we can do so here as well. Only one example in scripture of someone returning from the dead after being dead for a considerable length of time has direct bearing on our study. That example is discussed in the proceeding. Very few other examples of people being raised from the dead can be found, and all of them are in the New Testament. These people were raised from the dead almost immediately after they had passed. They were raised by either Jesus or the Apostles to give credibility to the Word they were preaching. For example, the raising of Tabitha and Lazarus were, according to scripture, performed to attest to the Lord's power over death and not a case of the dead reaching back to the living. These were special situations in which the dead were made alive again, not in which the dead reached back from the other side of the grave. For our study therefore, they cannot be considered applicable.

Let us consider the one example just alluded to, and since we have only this one actual example, we must understand it correctly. That account is found in 1 Samuel 28. Here Saul, the first king of Israel, in a contemptible act against God, had a witch call up the spirit of Samuel the Prophet. You may read the account if you wish, but the gist of the story is that it was an evil thing to do and God was not pleased. In 1 Samuel 15:23, Samuel, then still alive, specifically (and I believe providentially in anticipation of the events that would happen with the witch) admonished Saul about this sort of thing by stating, "For rebellion is as the sin of witchcraft." The prophet taught Saul that witchcraft was evil in the sight of God. God knew that Saul was going to contact the witch in the future and wanted to ensure that he was not ignorant and that his attempt to call up the dead would be viewed as an act of rebellion against God.

Saul knew this was taboo, and yet, he still contacted the witch. If you read the account, by her words and expressed concern, we see that even the witch knew it was wrong and feared reprisals for her part in it. And by the way, God is the one who allowed Samuel's spirit to speak that day and not the witch, to make his point. In fact, she knew that she had no such power but feared the king and went through the motions as she was told to do.

People simply cannot come back to earth at their own discretion or at the will of others. The Bible teaches throughout the New Testament that when we die, we are transported forever out of this world. When God removes us from this world, it is permanent and irreversible. The book of 2 Corinthians 5:8 tells us:

*To be absent from the body and to be present
with the Lord.*

Refer if you would please, to the book of Luke 16:19–31 in the New Testament. Here we have the account of a rich man and a beggar by the name of Lazarus. You should be familiar with this story as I used it earlier to make another point. We are told that both men died. The rich man wound up in torment in hell and the poor beggar was comforted in paradise by Abraham. They were in separate chambers of a place called Hades, but they were still able to see each other.

The rich man made two requests of Abraham: The first was that Lazarus might dip the tip of his finger in water and bring a drop to him to quench his thirst. The other request was that Lazarus might return to earth to warn the rich man's brothers about the terrible place he was in so that they might turn from their wickedness and avoid it. To both requests Abraham answered in the negative. No doubt Abraham was moved by the man's torment and by the plight of his brothers. It does not say that, but we know Abraham was a compassionate man by the way he had lived his life. He had always tried to intervene and help others, as with Lot, his nephew, in Sodom just before the destruction of that city. I am sure that he would have accommodated both requests if he had been able to do so. That notwithstanding, we see by his answer in verse 26 that people on the other side simply cannot visit the living even if their motives are selfless and good.

Throughout scripture you can find ample discouragement toward trying to contact the dead and overwhelming evidence that the dead, human or otherwise, are not at liberty to return to this life for a visit. When Mary came to the grave of Jesus, the angels asked, "Why seek you the living among the dead?" Their message was clear. Christ Jesus rose and was alive; he was no longer in the grave. He was no longer among the dead. So then, the dead can no longer be among the living. In essence, the dead are no longer dead when they leave this world, but alive in another place. They are not ghostly apparitions, but physical beings. The living of that place cannot visit the living of this place.

You must note that the angels were emphasizing a divide that exists between the living and the dead that cannot be trespassed. The dead are unreachable for us, and we are unreachable for them. I realize that there are mediums and spiritualists who claim to contact those who have passed over. Some are fakes to be sure, preying upon the emotional distress of grieving individuals. But some are not. No doubt there are those who are reaching someone beyond, but I assure you it is not who they think it is.

One of the biggest misconceptions people have concerns God's providence. People think that he is in control of everything. That simply is not true. Please do not misunderstand. God certainly is all-powerful and can control everything if he wants to. But he does not want to. God has two ways of dealing with things: First, there is his "providence." Providence is simply described as being the absolute and unchangeable will of God. He desires something to be and it is. Creation is a good example of this. "In the beginning God created." It simply happened because he wanted it to, and nothing and no one could have changed his will to do so. Second, is God's "permissive will." This is completely different from God's providence. By his permissive will, God permits things to happen, whether he personally approves of them or not, because he wants people to have choice and free will. He does not want us to be robots but free to make our own decisions. For example, he could force everyone to love him, but he does not because he prefers we willingly accept and love him.

The world, by God's permissive will, runs on automatic. In

other words, God does not cause everything that happens to happen; he merely allows it to. For instance, if a tree falls, it was not God who wielded the axe, but a man. There was cause and effect. By God's providence, both man and tree exist, but by his permissive will, one caused an effect on the other. Now the reason I point out this difference is that most people blame God for what goes on here on earth. In their minds everything bad happens because he wanted it to, and they justify this idea of God perpetrating evil on us by saying, "Well you know the Lord works in mysterious ways!" That just is not true. There is nothing mysterious about it at all. He may have "allowed" it to happen, but he certainly did not want it to.

Let me surprise many of you by stating that God is not the *god* of this world. I can hear you now, "What, are you nuts. What kind of simpleton are you anyway?" Whoa, before you throw this book into the trash and label me a heretic, let me explain. Yes, God created this world. Yes, he created people and animals and all the material things. And yes, he owns the world. But I am sure that you are aware that there are other forces at work here as well. You will note that in my startling statement just mentioned, the second time I used the word god, it was with a lowercase g. It was not a typo. It was on purpose. This is the lowercase word used to describe false gods in scripture. In 2 Corinthians 4:3–4, it is used to describe Satan. It says:

> But if our gospel be hid, it is hid to them that are
> lost: In whom the god of this world hath blinded
> the minds of them which believe not.

These verses do not require the services of a theologian to interpret, in respect to the point I am making. The meaning is straightforward and simple. This world is controlled by a god. Never does the Bible refer to the Almighty, whether in the person of the Father, Son, or Holy Spirit with a lowercase g. That designation is always used to identify false gods. In this case, it is the old devil himself, Satan. But unlike other false gods, Satan is a real being. All the other gods in scripture are nothing more than pieces of wood, stone, or fashioned metals. Often they are concoctions of human and animal form, derived from myth or legend. They have no life and no power.

Satan has both. There can be no doubt but that he has great power in this world. He also wields great influence and persuasive abilities. The Bible clearly shows that he has control here, in particular with the workings of this world (government, religion, schools, courts, etc.). Again, that is not to say that God has no power. In fact, he has absolute power. He merely allows Satan to exercise temporary control. There are several reasons for this, none of which apply to our study, so we will not give space to them here. Suffice it to say that this situation is allowed by God's permissive will, because it fits into his plan, and that this situation will change at exactly the time God desires it to, according to his providential will. Make no mistake, Satan's power is limited and temporary.

If there are still any doubts as to who currently has control of the world system, turn briefly to the letter written to the Ephesians, now forever preserved as the tenth book of the New Testament. In Ephesians 6, we are told that believers are in warfare

with unseen powers. Dark powers rule this world and wage warfare against the saints (believers) of God. We are told to stand
in our faith and to use the weapons God has provided for us for
the battle. The Apostle Paul delineates the weapons we have at
our disposal. You may read about those at your leisure, but I
want you please to note verses 11 and 12, for those powers are
clearly identified for us. It says:

> *Put on the whole armor of God, that ye may be*
> *able to stand against the wiles of the devil. For we*
> *wrestle not against flesh and blood, but against*
> *principalities, against powers, against the rulers of*
> *the darkness of this world, against spiritual*
> *wickedness in high places.*

Clearly, God is issuing a warning to us that there are evil
powers at work that we cannot see because they are not flesh
and blood. Satan is the "ruler of the darkness of this world" that
Paul the Apostle is speaking of. He is the foe of Christ. Consequently, he is the foe of Christians. Well for that matter, Satan
hates all people, but he especially hates Christians because we
know about him. He hates people because God loves them. He
has a hatred for anything that God loves because he hates God.
Simply stated, Satan hates what God loves and loves what God
hates. He wages war against the saints of God and wishes to
neutralize our lives so that we can do nothing for God. That is
why the Apostle Peter was compelled by the Lord to write to
believers in 1 Peter 5:8:

*Be sober, be vigilant; because your adversary the
devil, as a roaring lion, walketh about, seeking
whom he may devour.*

He is not a benign or passive ruler of darkness. Peter characterizes him as a roaring lion. He actively seeks to devour those who would follow God. He has extraordinary power and is capable of great corruption and evil. We need to realize this. His ability and power have been diminished in the minds of many by his characterization as a cute, red-suited man with horns, but he is absolutely and totally wicked. The danger he poses has been minimized by innumerable Hollywood movies that paint him in a harmless light and by the adoption of the humorous and dismissive phrase like those used by a sassy television personality of years gone by, for example, "The devil made me do it."

Satan has enjoyed painting for the world a self-portrait that masks his real personality. Despite these attempts to make him more palatable to the human race, however, he remains a considerable force of evil that we all need to recognize. If you have any doubts about the power of Satan or his resolve to perpetrate evil upon this world, you only need revisit the account of Jesus's temptation in the wilderness in chapter 4 of the book of Matthew.

Here, after the Lord had fasted for forty days, Satan moved swiftly to tempt him. Of course Satan failed, but notice that he had the power to take Jesus, the very Son of God, up to an exceedingly high mountain and showed him all the kingdoms of the world and said, "All these will I give thee, if thou wilt fall down and worship me." Note that Satan had to have had control of these kingdoms to make the offer. He said "I" will give them to thee. He is the "god" of this world.

Let me try to apply all that I have said here to the discussion at hand. If Satan was evil enough to try to tempt the Son of God and commanded power enough to show him all the kingdoms of the world, how is it that we are so reluctant to believe he can turn that power on us? Why is it we would rather believe that some experience we have in a very weak and emotional moment is everything it seems to be and not some wile of the devil? If, as I have shown, the Bible tells us that those who pass from this world cannot return and condemns the work of mediums and spiritualists, why is it that many are quick to still embrace the experiences they have had as authentic, over the sound teaching from the Word of God that rejects and denounces such experiences?

In case you were wondering, I acknowledge that the experiences are probably real. When someone writes to me and tells me that their pet, or at least the image of their pet, ran into the family living room and exited through a wall, I believe them. I know that the supernatural exists and they have no reason to lie. Admitting this, tasks me with the difficult challenge of reconciling what people are seeing to what is taught in the Bible. If people are not seeing their pets, then what is happening? Either the people are wrong or the Bible is. What is the answer? There can be only one answer: the answer is that the Bible is never wrong. But it is not that simple. Since the reports by people are believable, we have a conflict and we must find an explanation that reconciles these differences. And that answer must satisfy the supernatural considerations of these differences as well.

There can only be one plausible explanation. It must be that people are being deceived. Someone or something is taking advantage of their emotional moments and exploiting their time of vulnerability. That someone, of course, can be none other than the great deceiver, Satan, along with his league of demons. God makes it clear that the rulers of the darkness of this world can and do deceive. In fact, deceit is one of the primary things scripture tells us they are noted for. But this poses another difficulty. What would be the reason for this deception? Why would Satan bother to deceive people about anything, especially their pets? It seems so petty and senseless. What would motivate him, and what would be the payoff for him?

We find the answer in 2 Corinthians 11. Interestingly enough, what we read there also answers the questions as to why there are so many different religious beliefs in this world, why so many are deceived into following a way other than God's, and why Satan generally deceives on a grander scale rather than at the personal level. The Apostle Paul says of the gospel that there are those who would pervert the message of God and deceive those who would hear it. Specifically in verses 13–15 he says:

For such are false apostles, deceitful workers,
transforming themselves into the apostles of Christ.
And no marvel [wonder] for Satan himself is
transformed into an angel of light. Therefore it is
no great thing if his ministers also be transformed
as the ministers of righteousness; whose end
shall be according to their works.

Satan can and does transform himself into an angel of light in the eyes of people, and he also empowers those who serve him to appear to be ministers of light and righteousness. And the reason his motivation goes back to what I said earlier is that Satan hates what God loves and loves what God hates. It is his nature to imitate and deceive, and he cannot help himself. He hates people because they are made in God's image and are God's prized creation. He loves unrighteousness because he knows that God hates it. And he will use the temporal power he possesses to gratify himself in his hatred for God and the people God loves.

So how does this equate to his deceiving people about their pets? What possible benefit could Satan derive from comforting people with a false pet visitation? Obviously, one answer is that he cannot help himself. His nature is to be ungodly and to do sinful things. He likes being evil and hurting people. In addition, to coerce people into accepting exactly the opposite of what the Bible teaches must make him gleeful. It must satisfy his desire to do the things God hates. For people to believe other than God's Word causes God to be grieved. To have God grieve gratifies the wicked heart of Satan.

Finally, and I believe much more important to Satan, once he has people started down the road of religious error, this course of action makes it very easy for him to keep them on that path and to lead them deeper into the woods of religious confusion. Invariably, New Age writings are anti-Bible and, therefore, a tool to be used against God and against what is right. People are so quick to embrace the sensational and the fantastic. And Satan is eager to feed them whatever fantasy he can even if it means giving them temporal happiness and comfort by deceiving them into thinking their dear pet has come to visit. When people are searching for answers, when their hearts are tender due to their grief, they can be lured into believing their pets can visit them. Then, how hard will it be to sell other, more dangerous religiosity to them? I know how hard this is to accept. I know that some of you will balk at what I am saying because you have had your own supernatural experience, and you are thinking, "But I saw Sparky, it was real."

Remember, Satan displayed all the kingdoms of earth to Jesus. If he can conjure up the image of a kingdom, how easy is it for him to conjure up the image of one small animal? Remember, too, that there are biblical accounts of demons assuming animal forms or possessing animals, so this is not a baseless connection that I am trying to make. Satan has great power. He can appear to be a spirit or an angel of light. Is that not what some of you thought when you supposedly saw your pets, that they were spirits or angels?

Satan sometimes deceives by compromising, by giving temporal benefit or pleasure. He looks at the big picture. He wants to pull people away from God. He could not care less about our pets or us or about whether we are comforted in our pain, but if he can use our grief to confuse the bigger spiritual issues, he is willing to do so. I can only imagine that in his perverse economy, he can afford to give a little to gain a lot because he is pragmatic. If he can move people further away from God, he is willing to do whatever it takes, including offering up false comfort. If you get nothing else out of my words, please understand that.

Satan is a real being, with real powers. He hates you and he hates God, and anything he can do to hurt either or both, up to the point where God tolerates him doing so, he will do it. It is hard to believe that anyone could exploit the broken hearts of good people, but make no mistake, the evil one is capable of that and much, much more.

In John 8, he is called the liar. It doesn't say he is *a* liar, but *the* liar, indicating two things: he was the original liar, and he himself is the lie. When he tempted Eve, he lied to her. He is the utterly evil one, and what we count sacred, he does not. The Bible tells us that the spirit of the evil one is in the world today. That spirit is called the spirit of the Antichrist and he lies and deceives. Someday the actual Antichrist will be in power, but for now, his spirit influences this world. That spirit is the spirit of Satan. Let me just give you a helpful comparison of his spirit and the Spirit of our Lord, the Spirit of Truth, so that you might understand the deceitful resolve of this wicked being in his war against God and humanity.

Spirit of Truth (The Lord Jesus Christ)	Spirit of Error (The Antichrist)
Member of Holy Trinity (Father, Son, and Holy Spirit)	Member of Unholy Trinity (Satan, False Prophet, Antichrist)
Established His Church (the unspotted bride)	Establishes the Apostate Church (the great harlot)
Represents the Word of God	Misrepresents the Word of God
Came in God's name	Comes in his own name
He was despised by men	He will be exalted by men
He did his Father's will	He does his own will

Spirit of Truth	Spirit of Error
(The Lord Jesus Christ)	(The Antichrist)
He came to save mankind	He comes to destroy mankind
He is the Holy One	He is the Lawless One
He is the Son of God	He is the Son of Perdition
He is the sacrificial lamb	He is the ravenous wolf
He will glorify his bride the church	He will kill his harlot wife the false church
He is God who made himself man	He is man who will make himself god (lowercase g)
He represents the Spirit of truth	He represents the spirit of error
He loves man	He hates man
He will be exalted	He will be destroyed

In summary, I do not mean to put down those who have had an experience of the type we discussed earlier, and I certainly do not mean to strip those of the comfort they might have derived from such an experience. But knowing what the Bible says about such things and knowing the wicked tactics of that evil one, what kind of person would I be if I remained silent and let you cling to that deceit?

According to scripture, neither animals nor people can return to earth to visit. They cannot communicate with us. Disembodied spirits cannot move candles across a table or cause their voices to be captured on some hi-tech tape recorder as white noise. No so-called psychic or medium can reach them either. The Bible says they are unreachable. Now no doubt mediums and soothsayers are speaking to someone. They are indeed reaching the supernatural world. I will concede that. But they are not talking to whom they think they are talking to, and my advice would be for them to exercise extreme caution and for you to avoid them.

Bottom line, the spirits of departed pets cannot come back to visit for any reason. But this knowledge should not be a source of discouragement or sadness. They are well. They are happy. Should we lament the emergence of a beautiful butterfly from its cocoon? Should the blooming of a stunning flower cause us pain? Neither should the graduation of our devoted pet to a place of wonder and joy weigh heavily upon us. That they live on in a place as wonderful as heaven should be a reason for true joy and celebration.

Chapter 12

SIGNS AND MIRACLES

As I explained in the last paragraph of the previous chapter, one of the biggest problems I have detected with people who have these so-called ghost pet experiences is that they misinterpret what is happening. They consider their experience some sort of sign from God or a miracle. What is the sign about? What is miraculous about it? They do not know. They only know that it is a sign or a miracle. But is it?

Although I do not know most of my readers, I feel a responsibility to each to represent truth in what I write. I have a self-imposed debt I owe to them and to myself. I am very conscientious about this debt and pay great attention to the details to ensure that I display honesty and accuracy in all that I publish. In keeping with this, we are going to need to address a misconception people have regarding signs and miracles before we get to the real help promised in subsequent chapters.

Earlier, we looked at several of the experiences relayed to me by people who lost their pets. In the next two chapters, I am going to share some experiences where the people involved thought that they had witnessed a sign or miracle. I offer these neither in support of, nor opposition to, that perception, but rather to show how easy it is to misconstrue and mislabel such experiences. Besides, stories always make for good reading, so I am hoping you will enjoy them. The accounts have nothing to do with animals, but I hope they will serve to represent the misconception that exists about the signs and miracles I want to showcase. Although I have volumes of stories I could use that people have sent to me over the years, I am going to use personal stories from my own family's experiences to ensure that I do not violate anyone's privacy. I assure you that these are all true accounts and that I have not embellished in any way.

EXAMPLE I

In 1969, my Uncle Ted, who was a Catholic priest, passed away unexpectedly at the very young age of thirty-nine. I was serving in the United States Navy at the time and overseas aboard an aircraft carrier. As the custom or rule was in those days, unless it was "immediate" family, you were not allowed to return home, so I was not able to attend his funeral. My grandmother (my uncle's mother) and my own mother attended the funeral service. They sat together, but took turns visiting the open casket alone. Later, after the interment, they held each other and wept and shared the most amazing story with each other eventually. Almost simultaneously they reported to each other and the attending family that during each their visits to view his body, Uncle Ted had sat up in the casket, smiled, and said, "Don't worry, I'm okay," and then he returned to his prone position.

These reports, given independently of each other, despite giving us the willies, were quite encouraging and uplifting to the family. Things with a positive supernatural flavor usually are. This had happened years before I made a personal commitment to the Lord and knew what the Bible said about such things. So at the time, it made me somewhat excited, spiritually speaking. On some level I suppose stories like that reaffirm that there is a supernatural world and thus the existence of God to us.

Now as a Bible student who knows what God's position is on this sort of thing, I know that while the experience apparently happened (because I knew both my mother and grandmother to be persons of integrity), it could not have been my uncle who was speaking. I cannot speculate at this late date what Satan's motivation for deceit may have been at that time, but I do know that it made me think, "Hey, I'll be okay too when I die because my uncle is." In fact, nothing could have been further from the truth. It was not until I came to know Christ Jesus as my savior that I learned the Bible teaches I was definitely *not* okay. Nothing my uncle said could influence my own responsibility to God to reconcile with him.

So at the very least, that experience served to deceive me, my mother, and my grandmother into thinking something contrary to what the Bible teaches. And if I had not come to the knowledge of the truth five years later, when Larry took the time to teach me what the Bible actually says about a relationship with God, I might still be trusting in the wrong thing. No doubt, some are thinking I am trusting too much in the Bible, I am a fanatic, and I am probably too religious for my own good. Think about that for a moment. How can you trust too much in what God has said? If there ever truly was an expert on anything, especially the next life, certainly it is he. As for being a fanatic, I kind of like that label because the root word is "fan" and that is pretty much what I am. I am a fan of God. I do not get all crazy or demonstrative about my faith, but I have a joy and security I never had before.

What or who should I believe in lieu of God? Should I trust some visual experience? Jesus did not. When tempted by the devil, he quoted the Word of God. The experience did not influence him at all. If I have to make a choice, I am going to follow his example. I will not trust what I see or hear, but defer to the Bible and hold whatever thing I am considering up to its light to see if it is true or not. Some might think that I am putting my uncle down, but I am not trying to do that. The fact is, my uncle was long gone when this alleged experience took place. It was not he sitting up in the casket, either physically or spiritually. He had nothing to do with it.

I am not putting down my grandmother or mother either, who have themselves since passed on. They were merely targets of the deceit. It is Satan who deserved the discredit then; it is he who deserves the discredit now for the deceit being perpetrated on grieving folks. There is virtually no difference in his tactic then from now. He deceived then and he deceives now. He deceives.

EXAMPLE 2

In 1964, my older sister and I had overslept one Saturday morning. I do not mean to give you the idea that this was out of the ordinary by saying "One Saturday morning." Indeed, this was the norm for us. We were teenagers. On this particular Saturday morning, we arose a little later than usual, however. My grandmother (same grandmother as in the previous story) had been waiting for us to get up and immediately began cooking a late breakfast for us. She was always cooking for us; she was such a dear.

My mother was not around and that struck my sister and me as rather odd. Mom seldom left us at home without telling us where she was going and when she would return. She was not the kind of mom to let you sleep in either, so it was strange that she had left without opening the blinds, yanking off our covers, and setting the dog on us to lick our faces. But she had not done any of those things, and it was a bit unsettling and mysterious. My dad was not there either, but that was usual. He was in the navy then and always at sea or down at the base making sure the boat was still afloat (or whatever he did). He was a machinist mate and also a submariner. Either dictates more sea assignments than the normal sailor, but both together kept him underway or on board at the pier most of the time.

We asked our grandmother where my mother had gone, and she told us that it was a secret. That only heightened the mystery and our curiosity. It was not like "Lil" to keep something from us. She was a swell grandmother, the proverbial picture of permissiveness. She allowed me, rather encouraged me, to call her by her first name, spoiling me with every imaginable bakery delicacies, allowing me to do whatever I wanted, and then standing between her son (my dad) and me when it was spanking time for what I had done.

My sister and I pestered and nagged her to tell us where Mom had gone for the longest time, because that always worked with Grandmother. It did not work this time, however, and it really had us perplexed. Lil just never could tell us no. This was new and it had us really curious now. My sister came up with the idea to ask the Ouija board where Mom was. In the 1960s, everyone had either a Ouija board or a Magic Eight Ball fortune-teller thing. They were the fads, second only to the Beatles in our neighborhood. There was nothing openly sinister about these items in those days. They were sold as board game items in the local department stores. My sister kept ours in her room. We grabbed it and sat with it on the living room floor. We put the little triangular indicating device in the center of the board and asked, "Where is mom?" We put our hands on the indicator, and it actually began to move across the board.

I remember thinking at the time that my sister was making it move, because I knew I was not doing it. She confided in me later that she was thinking that I had been moving it, because she knew she was not. Those suspicions were not to last. The indicator moved from letter to letter surprisingly quickly, spelling out G-R-A-N-D. We were thinking that it would spell out GRANDPA because my grandfather, my mother's father, lived only a few blocks away and Mom often would stop in to see him. When it continued and added M-A, however, we said defiantly, almost in concert, "No way, Grandma is in the kitchen." Then, when it continued to move and spelled G-R-A-N-D-M-A-V-A, It made no sense to us at all, and we lost interest in it. We pushed away from the game accusing each other of having pushed the indicator.

About an hour later, my mother came home and we ran to

her and asked where she had been and why Grandmother could
not tell us. She said, "I told Grandma not to tell you that I was
just down the street visiting your Great Grandma Vargo's grave.
I didn't want you running down there to find me. I wanted to
be alone."

I was too young to have very much hair on my neck, but what
ever peach fuzz was there was standing on end. My sister turned
pale white and we both were trembling. We knew by our respective reactions that neither of us had been forcing the Ouija
board. Somehow, someway, that board was spelling out Grandma
Vargo! It was very, very scary and unsettling. That was actually
our first realization that there really was a spirit world. Inevitably,
along with that realization came an understanding that God ac
tually did exist, that Satan also was real, and that there were powers at work that we knew nothing about. I had no idea whether
the force behind the board was evil or good, but I really did not
care. I was never going to touch that board again!

It was a startling discovery for a teenager, and I have never
forgotten that day. But, in retrospect, that very scary and negative experience also served a good purpose in my life. The realization that there is another, unseen world has been a positive
fuel in the faith I embrace today. Both my sister and I were void
of any real Bible knowledge back then. Neither of us had any
idea what it all meant and why it happened. We both dismissed
it and moved on, although the frightfulness of the moment stayed
with us. Today as a man who knows his Bible and who has experienced firsthand the deceit of the wicked one, I have little
doubt that what we tapped into was a demon.

Ouija boards are tools of the occult and mediums. On the surface there appears to be no danger, often nothing happens, but when you do get them to work, you get what is advertised—a supernatural experience. Obviously, since these are tools of dark forces and people receive guidance from them, they are opening themselves up to great deceit and tremendous spiritual problems. One must note here that some of the people who contacted me about their experiences also had consulted a Ouija board prior to that experience. Is this a coincidence? I doubt it.

Now then, while these two examples are not exactly representative of the types of experiences people share with me in relation to pets that have passed on, they do serve to illustrate the supernatural power that is at work in this world and the methods and tools employed against people in an effort to deceive. They also serve to establish the premise for our discussion on the purpose of this chapter—signs and miracles.

To preclude confusion, I think we need to define what we mean when we use the words "sign" and "miracle" in a spiritual context? There is a wide spectrum of meaning assigned to these terms. Too many people use these words interchangeably, when, in fact, they do not mean the same thing at all. For the purpose of our study, let us keep it biblical and simple. A sign is simply a signal or token from God sent for any number of reasons to confirm something he has covenanted, promised, or said. For example, God spoke to the shepherds through his angelic host and told them "And this shall be a sign unto you, you shall find the babe wrapped in swaddling clothes and lying in a manger." The effect of the sign was that when the shepherds found the babe in the manger wrapped in swaddling clothes, they would know that this was the Christ child God had told them about and the one who had been prophesied about for so many centuries.

A miracle is not the same as a sign. A miracle is simply described as a specific and deliberate act of God that is both extraordinary and that lacks natural explanation. A miracle always has purpose and always means to bring attention or glory or both to God. Signs are an attesting to the recipient that God has done or will do what he has promised. A miracle is the doing of that thing God gave a sign for. The sign was the shepherds were to find the babe as God had said; the miracle was that the babe was God in the flesh, born of a virgin.

Admittedly, these are my definitions and not that of Mr. Webster, but I believe they capture the essence of the understanding of these words held by most people who are familiar with the Bible and the words and works of God. I am sure others could come up with better definitions, but these will serve our purpose.

A sign is not always extraordinary. It usually is something special, but not always extraordinary. Accepting a sign at face value requires a modicum of faith. Consequently, if we ponder a sign long enough, our logic can and usually will explain it away. A miracle is not so easily dispatched. Miracles have no explanation and require no faith. To deny what our eyes have beheld is difficult. Seeing is believing. That signs require faith is perhaps the reason God did not indulge people with signs that often. Certainly, he used them as in our example of the shepherds and the manger. A sign was needed. There may have been many babies born in Bethlehem during that time, but there was only one baby born in Bethlehem who was wrapped in swaddling clothes and lying in the manger that evening, the baby Jesus.

God uses signs throughout the Bible to reveal things to people, to signal that his hand is upon a thing. But one must note that God himself discourages people from looking for a sign. You may study this out in depth at your leisure, but for convenience sake, I will try to explain why God takes this position.

In Matthew 12:38, the scribes and Pharisees questioned Jesus's authority when they asked:

Master, we would see a sign from thee.

They wanted to know who Jesus was. More accurately, they wanted him to tell them who he thought he was. They wanted to trap him by having him give some heretical answer they could accuse him of. They wanted to know by what authority he did the things he did, and the way they presented that challenge to his authority was to seek a sign. They tried to set him up for failure.

Jesus responded to the representatives of these religious sects in verse 39 and said:

An evil and adulterous generation seeketh
after a sign.

Now why would Jesus say something like this? Clearly, if you look at the context of this passage and others like it, you will see that God considers the demanding of a sign from him an expression of doubt in whom he is and the authority he possesses as God the Creator.

Think back to the times you have asked God to send you a sign. What compelled you? What was your motivation? I can tell you what motivated me. I was hurting or in trouble or scared, and I wanted God to give me a signal that he was real, that he was still on the job, that he was aware of my situation, and that he was able to do something about it. By asking for a sign, I manifested my doubts about him. If he were real (and I was not really sure), then I would want him to let me know and reassure me. I reasoned that if he could just give me a sign that he was there, I would be okay.

Isn't that really what asking for a sign is—expressing doubt in God even if just for a moment? I wonder how that makes him feel? I know how I feel when someone doubts something I say especially because I pride myself on being an honest person. I can understand therefore, how a perfect and holy God feels when someone doubts him. In Luke 11:16, it tells us:

> And others tempting him; sought of him a
> sign from heaven.

Jesus was not pleased with them. He knew in their hearts that they doubted his authority and were just mocking him. Later in this same chapter, in verse 29, he responds to their doubt and says:

> This is an evil generation: they seek a sign; and
> there shall no sign be given it

Jesus was not going to play their game. He was not going to feed their unbelief. One would think that the giving of a sign would strengthen the recipient's faith, but it seems just the opposite is true: if your doubt requires validation via a sign, your unbelief will find a natural explanation for the sign and potential faith will be influenced negatively rather than positively.

Is it any wonder that God does not entertain our desires to see signs? Catering to our requests would have a detrimental effect, whether we understand that it would or not. It would lead to stronger disbelief. We are not told this, but it would not surprise me to learn that one or more of the shepherds eventually started questioning the sign they were given. It is just human nature, and God understands this better than we do.

I do not mean to belabor the point about signs, but I feel compelled to add that another reason God discourages our looking for signs may be that people are prone to trying to make deals with God while asking for a sign. By discouraging the desire to look for signs, God perhaps hopes the practice of making deals can also be discouraged. I do not know what it is about us humans, but we all fall prey to the desire to deal with God as if he were some game show host. I admit that I have been guilty of such behavior. Have you not? When the chips are down, when we are at wit's end corner, we turn to God and say something like "God, if you will just let this happen in my life, then I'll do such and such for you."

I could write another book on what the Bible has to say on this subject. Significant guidance is available as well as no shortage of examples of people who tried to make deals with God, who utterly and miserably failed to keep their end of the bargain that they unilaterally made without God's agreement. God is not in the business of making deals with people. We may think that he is, but he is not. That is a clear teaching from the Bible. There are many accounts of people attempting to make deals with God, but I cannot think of one that was successful. In fact, several led to tragedy. However, that would take us off point, and I do enough of that by accident without having to do it on purpose.

And that point is this: that we will inevitably follow the attempt to make a deal with God with something like "Can you give me a sign that you agree Lord," which further demonstrates to God our unbelief and doubt. God says that when we pray, we should do so in faith, nothing wavering. Making a deal and asking for a sign are not expressions of faith. Since requiring a sign usually results in one trying to make a deal with God, you can understand how God historically used signs sparingly, and then usually only when it served his purposes as with the angels and the shepherds.

Whether the need be water for a failing crop, healing of a loved one, or getting relief from grief over the loss of a pet, most of us are inclined to seek signs and make deals with God. It is our nature to do so. It is within us. The truth be known, even professing atheists will try to make a deal with God when they are at wit's end corner. It is just something we humans do.

I think I have made the point clear on signs. Now is the time to make the transition to miracles. A sign can be logically dismissed; a miracle cannot. Many in science have often tried to explain biblical miracles away with their brand of rationale, but unsuccessfully. Miracles, by definition, are unexplainable. A miracle is something completely different from a sign, and I think much more apropos to the evaluation of the experiences that pet people are reporting. Some hazard a guess that God is sending them some sort of sign that their pets are okay. Again, that is not the purpose of a sign by Bible definition, so I cannot align myself with that thinking.

If I were going to choose between sign and miracle, I would lean more toward miracle. However, I am not saying that they are experiencing miracles either. Miracles are unexplainable, and as I have shown previously, I believe this phenomenon is explainable. Please do not misconstrue my position. I definitely believe in miracles, but we may differ as to what qualifies as a miracle. To me, each new day, each bird singing, each newborn, and each sunrise is a miracle. My ability to feel the heat of the sun, to hear rushing water, and to witness a sunrise or sunset are all miracles of this wonderful life that God has given to me.

Of the billions of planets and stars we have been able to search, no other place is like Earth. Earth is a miracle. Scientists keep saying that there are, but they still have not found one. We have been able to look at billions of stars and planets, and no evidence is found of life anywhere else. On the other hand, Earth is life packed. It is wonderfully and masterfully balanced to support life, despite all our efforts to destroy it. Earth is a miracle by design, not by chance. From the time two people walked in a pristine garden to today's nearly seven billion souls, the earth has continued to work the way it was designed.

Life itself is a miracle. The intricacies of our bodies are extraordinary. In thousands of years of study, scientists still do not understand it all. They tell us that our bodies are nothing more than water, calcium, and a few other elements, worth only about one dollar at face value, but no one has made a multimillion dollar machine that can function as perfectly. In Psalms 139:14, the Psalmist wrote:

I am wonderfully and fearfully made.

The complexities of the systems of our bodies: the nervous system; the circulatory networking of hundreds of thousands of miles of arteries, veins, capillaries, and so on; the cleansing agents and free radicals that automatically do their jobs to clean and protect our blood; endorphins; the senses of vision, hearing, taste, and so on, are miracles every one. And to think, God did all that with just a dollar's worth of water and calcium! A team of our best engineers, scientists, and doctors could not come close to duplicating or reproducing the human body. Can anyone deny how miraculous an event reproduction is? Sure science can duplicate the womb and nurture a fetus, but they must start with the ingredients God provided. A real test would be for them to create their own egg and sperm, but they cannot.

What about the biggest miracle of all? How is it possible that God can love this lump of calcium and water? Because within the skin of this lump of clay, he placed a mind and a heart, not the fleshy organs in our head and chest, but our consciousness, our emotions, our place of reason and logic, and our personality. All of this together we know as the soul. All of it is a miracle.

So many things qualify as miracles. However, I suppose I should confine myself to the type of miracles I know readers are interested in at the moment. But it is so hard to speak of miraculous things and not reflect on some of the genuine miracles of

God that we take for granted each and every day. Nevertheless, let me turn my thoughts to the kind of miracles I promised to discuss or at least to what those who write to me consider miracles. These would be the reported visions of departed pets in some of their homes and the dreams people have. We already have determined from scripture that the Bible does not support phenomenon that I labeled ghost pets. Still, something is definitely happening, we cannot deny that. And whatever is happening seems to be miraculous, but is it?

One disclaimer: You need to understand a very important yet often overlooked fact about miracles and that is that miracles are not always from God. In fact, I will go out on a limb and say that most miracles, at least the sensational and extraordinary events we call miracles today, are not from God. Does that shock you? It probably does because most people jump to the conclusion that when something extraordinary happens, it has to be from God. After all, he is the Almighty. He alone has great power.

Jumping to that conclusion is nothing to be embarrassed about. It is natural to think that way. We usually credit sensational and extraordinary events to God. But the fact is, Satan has the ability to perform miracles as well. Perhaps, we would be more accurate calling them antimiracles, but since the Bible does not assign such a label, I will not either.

The devil is allowed a certain amount of power by God. But make no mistake, God retains absolute control over everything. Nothing happens without his knowledge and permission. Satan's power is temporary and someday God will strip him of it. We cannot afford to go into detail here, but briefly, before man's advent, God gave Satan (then known as the archangel Lucifer) authority over this earth. He will not rescind that authority until Jesus's return to earth. Until then, there is a plan that must unfold.

Pending the arrival of that time and subject to the restraints God places on him, Satan has considerable power, and he uses it to further his evil goals, whatever they may be. Remember, he showed Jesus the kingdoms of the world. What was the purpose of doing this? Was it to help Jesus? No, it was just Satan being himself and trying to undermine or thwart the providence of God. Again, though it may not appear to be so, Satan is greatly restrained for perpetrating evil on humanity. There is a time coming, however, known to Christians as the Great Tribulation when the restraints will be removed.

During the period of Tribulation, Satan will amaze the world with his power through the person of the Antichrist. It will be a time unparalleled in human history and a time when all will see the true character and power of the wicked one. His power will be stunning, unlike anything the modern world has ever seen, but even then, it will be limited. Satan is not equal to God. He is not omniscient, not omnipotent, and not omnipresent. He cannot read our minds and he cannot foretell the future. But he has great power and authority in our world. He has been around for a long time, and he knows human nature and knows how to deceive us successfully. Satan also empowers those who follow his evil leadership. His demons tap into his power and are typically deceitful and self-serving. In the gospels we have many accounts of demonic power, for instance, the maniac of Gadara, a man possessed of a group of demons known as Legion.

According to the Bible, there are immense numbers of demons, perhaps billions—but certainly millions. They are still at work in the world today. They have an agenda, and that agenda is to deceive and to do spiritual harm to humankind. Many of my contemporaries suggest that the reason Satan and his horde deceive is that they believe if they can keep enough of the human race from reconciling with God, God will have to recant his judgment on them. It is the "safety in numbers" philosophy. This could very well be their motivation, but I am inclined to believe that the reason for their evil ways is their evil way. In other words, they are wicked and deceitful by nature and know no other way. The Bible refers to these wicked creatures as "natural brute beasts." It is natural, or their nature, to be the way they are.

It is like an adult bull moose in the wild during mating season: you do not have to do anything to upset it except be present in its world. Its very nature causes it to want to hurt you. You can talk soothingly to it, offer it some choice grass or sugar cubes, and try your best to get along with it, but it is going to chase you down and stomp on you. That is its nature. The same is true with Satan and his demonic following: all we have to do is be in their presence and they want to harm us. We are God's prized creation. They hate God and they hate us.

And then there are his human followers. They also have a modicum of his power available to them. Look at the contest between Pharaoh and Moses in the book of Exodus when the magicians of Egypt duplicated some of the miraculous feats God did through Moses. Those who delve into the occult and black arts can sometimes find a certain amount of power available from the one they serve.

Hollywood has capitalized heavily on the supernatural and the

wickedly miraculous. They have hyped up evil so much that people have become numb to the danger and consider the supernatural nothing more than fodder for television and movies.
People do not fear evil as they once did. This mindset has found
its way into many churches. Today you seldom hear anything
from the pulpit about evil and wickedness. Evil is almost acceptable, even familiar. The prevailing message is that God is
love and that is all we need to know. Now there is nothing wrong
and everything right with communicating God's love, but when
you do so to the exclusion of warning people about evil, you are
not giving people a level playing field.

There is evil in this world, wicked, deceitful evil. That evil
wants to confuse and mislead the masses. It uses the propensity
of people to gravitate toward the miraculous and supernatural
against them. If the evil one were to dress up his deceit to appear Godly and glorious and if he were to touch the heart of individuals and make them think they are receiving some special
privilege from God to see their little buddy one more time, it
would be so much the better for his quest to mislead.

I suppose the question needs to be asked, why do people gravitate toward the supernatural? Why did hundreds flock to see a
grease spot on the wall of an auto repair shop in Brownsville,
Texas, that reportedly looked like the virgin Mary (as if anyone
could tell you what she looked like)? Why do tens of thousands
go to a little city in Georgia each year allegedly to see a statue
bleed?

I suspect, and think you will agree, that we humans are a superstitious lot. Some will say "I'm not superstitious" and perhaps you aren't, but that does not mean you are not influenced

by superstition. Be honest, how many times have you broken a mirror and thought, Oh no. Were you thinking of the bad luck myth, even though you really did not believe it? How many times have you decided not to walk under a ladder? Oh, you told yourself it was because it was dangerous, but we both know the truth. We are all just a little too superstitious.

Good people, intelligent people, logical people can be influenced by superstition without even realizing it. Often we mix our religion and superstition together. For instance, I once lived in a zip code that started with the numbers 666. When people asked me for my zip code on the telephone, you could cut the silence with a knife when I answered them with, "It is 66614." They didn't hear the last two digits, just the 666.

Frequently, after the initial shock, they would reply "Uh, ah, um, you're kidding right, you do know what those numbers mean?" Now did these people think that I was living in a town called Hell with the Antichrist as mayor? Of course they didn't. But they could not help but associate the number 666 with the Bible use of that number. And in their minds, they added a smattering of superstition. By superstitious I mean that they add more urban legend to the number 666 than the Bible calls for. There is nothing evil about the number six in and of itself. If that were true, we would have to eliminate the number from our entire numbering system. The fact is that the Bible says that the number 666 is the number of a man. I suspect that is because six is the number most associated with humankind in the Bible. Humankind was created on the sixth day, told to work six days, given an earthly history that will have spanned six dispensations, and so on. But those who do not possess a firm grasp of the scriptures sometimes assign superstition to the things that they do not fully understand.

If being superstitious was not bad enough, we humans also like to sensationalize the things we fear or do not understand. It just makes it more fun when a story has a little more "pizzaz" to it. The media and the masses are quick to buy into the hype and help a thing grow larger than it actually is. People like the sensational. Take for example darkness. There is nothing inherently evil about the darkness, in and of itself. To be sure, most people prefer light to darkness. We find going places and doing things in the dark harder than doing them in the light because of reduced visibility. For that reason, more crimes are committed in the darkness than in the light, but that is because people are evil, not the darkness. They merely use the cloak of darkness to do their dastardly deeds.

Knowing this, our imagination sometimes kicks in, and we are much more apprehensive of the dark than perhaps we should be. Again, nothing is evil about darkness, but that does not keep us from imagining that evil. There is just "something" about the dark and we all feel it. The news media and Hollywood sensationalize the dangers of darkness and dress it up with a cloak of fear and superstition. Knowing that it is our nature to fear the dark and that we are intrigued by the supernatural and mysterious, they tap into those primal fears and continue to create a steady stream of chiller movies and television series for us to consume. The monsters and ghouls they have concocted over the years have never, do not now, and will never exist, but that does not keep us from fearing them when we are in the element of darkness. Again, there is just something about the dark, and you know it.

Most horror movies are set in scenes of darkness to create the right mood and mindset. This plays upon the natural apprehensions we have about the dark. No doubt this sells more products for Hollywood, but it also helps us enjoy the movie more. We don't go to see scary movies to laugh or feel romantic. The scarier it is, the better it is. There's something about the dark that makes it better.

Scary stories are not usually told in the bleachers at a softball game on a hot day. They are best delivered in the dark around a campfire. The dancing shadows created by the light fighting back the darkness of the forest enhance the story, and sometimes they make the evil character come to life. I cannot recall one time having my scoutmaster or others tell spooky stories during the daytime hours. No, those sensational stories were saved for a time after the sun went down for effect. Now in retrospect with an adult perspective, I can see how those stories served to help keep us youngsters in our sleeping bags rather than wandering the forest. The scoutmaster knew that there was something about the dark.

Now I do not care who you are, how tough you are, or what your occupation is. You may be a firefighter, a police person, a person who trains lions, or a race car driver. You may jump out of planes for a hobby or tag alligators as I used to do. You may have mastered the fears of your profession or hobby that you routinely face. It does not matter. When it comes to facing the dark, the bravest, the strongest, and the ones with nerves of steel, all have at least some apprehension that they do not have in the light.

When your family is out of town and you turn off the lights in your own home at night, a place you are very familiar with, why is it that you hear creaks and snaps and other eerie sounds that you do not remember hearing when the lights were on? There is something about the dark and something about being alone in it that makes a body more apprehensive. How is it that walking that cheerful, familiar street in the daylight is a completely different experience than when walking it at night? I have said it a half-dozen times now: there is just something about the dark, is there not? We have been conditioned to embrace superstition and to fear the dark. We are all afraid of the dark on some level. It is our nature and I am no different. I had to sleep with a light on as a child and all the closet doors had to be shut. If I had been able to convince my mom, the doors would have all been nailed shut before the sun went down. I knew the insides of my closets well in the daytime, and there was nothing to fear inside of them. But at night, monsters of every size and shape found their way in through hidden passages and panels in the walls.

Of course, there were no monsters. It was merely my natural fear of the dark at work, exacerbated by the hype of Hollywood and the media to sensationalize the dark and associate it with the supernatural. Moreover, I was not the exception. Kids everywhere felt as I did about this thing called darkness. For children, and to a lesser degree adults, the strong character strengths we display during daylight are not as readily available in the darkness. Often reason will succumb to imagination, courage will compete with apprehension, and a sound mind will give way to panic. Perhaps, this true account of something that happened to me as a child will remind you of a similar experience in your life.

I had a friend over to spend the night when I was ten years old. We were sent to bed early, but we talked and laughed for hours and entertained ourselves by standing up on the bed and looking out the open window that faced San Francisco Bay. We lived right on the bay at Hunter's Point Naval Shipyard, directly across from Candlestick Park. There must have been a football game that evening as the stadium was all aglow. We could hear cheering and music. It was just as well that we were staying up late and talking for no one could sleep through the racket the fans were making. Even though the stadium was nearly three miles across the bay from where I lived, there was nothing to block the sound as it wafted across the calm waters.

Later that evening, after the park had closed down, a quiet settled over the bay and we began to drift off to sleep. It had been a long day and we were tired. Suddenly, we were jolted to consciousness by a strange sound outside my window. Since we had been semiconsciously near sleep, we were not exactly sure what we heard, only that it was loud and awakened us. Though terrified (hey, we were only ten!), we slowly and cautiously stood up on the bed to look out of the window to see if we could identify the source of the noise. The street was dark and seemed deserted. All the automobiles that we could see were unoccupied. The water was quietly lapping up onto the shore on the other side of the road. The stadium was darkened and apparently closed. There was no indication of what the noise might have been. It was still and quiet.

Suddenly, to my horror, out of the corner of my eye, I saw the silhouettes of two men trying to climb into the house through the window on the opposite side of my bedroom. I do not know if my friend saw them, but that was not my immediate concern. My heart froze. I wanted to scream, but nothing would come out. I managed to regain my composure in a few seconds and started to lean toward the door. I was going to jump and dash to safety while alerting my dad.

As I started to lean, one of the men perceived my intentions and leaned with me, ready to pounce to catch me if I made that move. I made the move. As I did, the man jumped to chase me. It seemed he had jumped clear through the open window without any difficulty at all, landed on the floor soundly despite it being very dark, and was in very hot pursuit.

In fact, he was so quick, though only a split second had passed, it seemed he had managed to cross the entire room and almost had me in his grips. Realizing I did not have a chance, I froze again, stopping dead in my tracks. Oddly, so did the man. He stopped almost as quickly as I had. Maybe my dad had come into the room and the man saw him. I looked quickly to see, but the door was still closed. Dad had not come in. Turning back, the man had not moved. Then I realized that something was wrong, something was very wrong. Though I was in a panic, I had the presence of mind enough to realize suddenly that there were no other windows in my room. The only one was the one my friend and I had been looking out of. The glow from the moon was shining off the water through my window and projecting a false window on the wall across the room.

There were no men. The shadowy figures I thought were men climbing in another window were actually the shadows of my friend and me at the only window in the room. I suddenly understood what it meant to be "afraid of your own shadow." I felt so stupid, especially when my friend broke the silence by asking, "What the heck are you doing, Gary?" Apparently, he had seen the shadows and knew them to be shadows. He had not been panicked over the shadows, but was a bit concerned about my five seconds of bizarre behavior.

There is just something about the dark, is there not? Something that makes us superstitious, something we do not understand. If yielding to our natural fear is not enough, we also like to sensationalize and embellish upon the things we do not understand. We like to blow them way out of proportion to give them more excitement. Let me illustrate that with another true story from my life.

This time the story takes place primarily in broad daylight. I know you are probably thinking, But I thought you were talking about darkness? Actually, no, that was not the point I was trying to make. I am trying to evidence the peculiarity humans have to mix the supernatural and superstition together to sensationalize an experience. Darkness was just one of the ways we manifest that peculiarity. This second story has nothing to do with darkness, but it does speak to the peculiarity. This story was relayed to me by my late brother-in-law, Bert. He used to hunt wild pigs in the mountains of Oahu, Hawaii, where we lived. Without supporting or condemning that practice (because that is not the issue), I simply want to share the story.

Like the rest of us, Bert had his shortcomings, and once in a while he would embellish to make a story sound better than it was. When he did that, however, it was easy to tell, and when challenged, he would always grin and admit to stretching the truth a little. On this occasion, Bert was very serious as he relayed the details to me, and no amount of chiding or taunting could get him to budge on any part of what he told me.

Bert's story is about a hunting trip that he and some friends had taken a day earlier in a mountainous region near Schofield Barracks on the Island of Oahu. They were near Kolekole Pass, the place where Japanese aircraft came through the mountains to make their approach to Pearl Harbor over seven decades ago. Though much of this area is now restricted for federal use, some places are open for public use where hog hunting has proven to be very fruitful.

Late in the afternoon, their dogs caught the scent of a hog. They allowed the dogs to run and followed as closely behind them as they could. When they finally caught up with the baying hounds, the dogs were all positioned in a semicircle around a large thicket at the end of a box canyon. The dogs were growling with lowered heads as dogs often do when they are excited and apprehensive at the same time. The men were getting ready to flush out whatever was in the thicket, when all of a sudden there was a loud crashing sound as the bushes directly in front of them parted and something "big" came running out.

According to all the men present, they saw the bushes move and heard what sounded like a boar's heavy, angry breathing and snorting, but no animal was to be seen. The dogs, with back hair bristling, backed off from the bushes a few steps and moved closer together to create an obvious collective defensive posture.

Something had them spooked badly. Ordinarily, the dogs would be hard to restrain from diving into the bushes and securing whatever poor creature happened to be there. But that was not happening. They were very nervous.

From the way the dogs were acting, the men began to get nervous. They grew progressively more unsettled, barking (pardon the pun) questions and orders at each other:

"Brudda, what you see?"

"Nuttin', what you see?"

"Me too, nuttin."

"You go shake da bush, cousin!"

"You crazy cus, you go shake em!"

I apologize that it gets a little disgusting here, but I have to provide all the details if you are going to get the whole picture. The story continues that someone in the group grabbed one of the dogs and scooped the maka piapia out of the dog's eye and wiped it as best they could into his own eyes.

Maka piapia is the Hawaiian word for the goop that collects in the corner of a dog's eye. Legend has it that rubbing maka piapia into one's eye will allow a person to see the spirits the way some people believe that dogs can naturally see them. So after smearing this "yuk" in his eyes, the man turned pale, backed up slowly a few steps, turned, and took off running, yelling *"Devil pig, devil pig, run!"*

Unfortunately, that is the end of the story because apparently everyone heeded the warning and ran, including the dogs. No one else saw the devil pig that the man in question saw or rather allegedly saw, and he would not talk about the experience because another Hawaiian legend makes it taboo to tell what one sees when it comes to spiritual things. How very convenient. Now, do I believe this account? I absolutely do not. I do believe that these men believe it though. The men undoubtedly believed the individual who shouted out the warning to them about the devil pig because they all ran and did not stop running until they were back at their vehicle. I also believe that things happened just about the way they reported them happening. But I also believe (and know) that Hawaii is a land given to much spiritualism and folklore. People are very superstitious there. Sometimes, people are predisposed to believe something no matter what the facts are.

I am not sure what he may have seen, if anything, but this type of story is so common on the islands that you come to understand that it is almost required that one have such a story in order to have credibility and standing with his or her other superstitious friends. If you have visited Hawaii, you surely have heard the legend of the goddess Pele not allowing you to bring pork across the island of Oahu on the old road leading to Kaneohe; or the stories of the Menehune, Hawaii's answer to the leprechaun; or the scores of other urban legends that make up local folklore.

Local people are inclined to share these stories, accentuating the sensational, perhaps even spicing the story up a bit at times. The history of the Hawaiian Islands is a blend of facts, spiritualism, religion, and folklore. You will find no shortage of those who will embellish on the legends that come from this blend.

The Hawaiians are a sweet and kind people, and they would never embellish maliciously. They are just superstitious.

The bottom line is, I did not then and do not now believe the story. I have no idea what a devil pig is anyway. I know first-hand how aggressive and even deadly big wild boars can be, but I have never seen one that looked like a devil. Moreover, I have a problem attaching credibility to anyone who is dumb enough to rub a dog's eye goop in his or her own eyes. They just are not clicking on all cylinders. I mean no disrespect to my brother-in-law or his friends. We all like to spice up our stories a little. They just went a bit too far in their superstitions for my tastes.

All this is offered to make my point that people sometimes mix the supernatural and superstition together to sensationalize the effect. If we will do this when we are faced with the things of the dark or things of superstition, is it so hard to understand that we will do the same thing when we encounter something extraordinary or special, like a dream or alleged vision of a departed human or animal loved one? It should not be.

People love to add sensation to things that happen. In times of stress and emotional despair, we usually seek extraordinary help and set lofty expectations. When we feel broken and alone as we do when we lose a precious pet who has meant so much to us, we are quick to look for some sign from above that our best friend is okay and lives on. Is it unusual that we, who love our pets as if they were our own children, would beg God for a miracle and even try to make a deal with him to bring them back to life or at least give us a sign that they are okay? Of course it is not. In fact, from the many thousands of letters I have received, I can say that it is quite common and no one needs to feel any shame for having such ideas or thoughts. The problem is that this opens us up to potential deception in the ways I described earlier. We are quick to label anything that happens out of the ordinary as a miracle from God, and if we ask God for a miracle to begin with, we will believe whatever we receive to be from him. That does not mean that it is.

Now I can finally get to the part of this study that I have been working toward, the part that for me is most important. I know that I have taken the long way to get to this point, but sometimes you do not want to float a boat until you have all the holes plugged. I found many holes for me to plug before I got to this juncture. I had a lot of foundational truths to cover to ensure that what I am now going to say would make sense to you from a biblical perspective and also preclude my contemporaries from labeling me a heretic. Had I just jumped into it, most readers would have had too many questions on their mind to allow them to focus on what I am about to say. I wanted to remove that potential impediment by addressing those questions first because I do not want there to be any confusion about what I am going to say about miracles. I think you are ready for this now—and it is this:

God No Longer Performs Public Miracles.

If I had not gotten your ire up previous to this, no doubt I would now. You are not alone in your feelings of disdain for me; many of my fellow ministers will bitterly disagree with me. But before you (or they) condemn me, let me add that he still performs private miracles (although I will call them by another name shortly). This concept of public and private miracles no doubt will confuse some of you. For others, it may provoke questions about some of the things that happen in the religious organizations you belong to. I can think of several valid denominational and doctrinal questions that I would have asked years ago if I had been told what I just told you.

What I say in the following should answer the lion's share of them, without I hope offending anyone. My purpose in this book is not to cast doubt on anyone's religious beliefs or affiliations. I realize that may be a by-product, but it is not my purpose. My intention is simply to help those in need of answers, and I hope to frame their experiences in a way they can understand them. I have fashioned what I say to meet those goals and not wander into the area of denominational and doctrinal differences. If a reader feels so inclined to contact me via the provided e-mail address with questions on other points, I am both prepared and willing to discuss them anytime, but I do not do so in these pages. So please know that I am not standing on a soapbox now. What I have to say is very important so that you get the whole thrust of this book. Please read on.

Now then, what do I mean by public miracles? If you are familiar with the Bible or have ever attended Sunday school on a fairly regular basis, then you know that there are scores and scores of accounts in both the Old and New Testaments that describe public miracles. For those readers who may not have had those opportunities, a public miracle is simply an extraordinary event as we have defined earlier, performed in public and usually to benefit part or all of the public, but always to bring glory to God and to advance his plan. The miracle did not always have to be a spectacular event, just something that clearly was performed by God.

An example is any one of the many lepers in scripture who were healed and made whole. The miracle was performed in public. Witnesses saw a person, previously an outcast from society and called *unclean, unclean,* have his or her skin made smooth and free from disease in mere seconds. There was no magic elixir, salve, or ointment; the person healing the leper called upon God, and by faith was healed, immediately and permanently.

It certainly was a benefit to the leper, being cleansed from a dreadful disease, but the local public was also benefited and gave praise to God. They were uplifted by witnessing this miracle, and their faith was given a big shot in the arm. They shared the joy of the leper. Both the healed leper and the many who witnessed the healing derived benefit from the miracle, and God was given glory (praised) for his mercy. In every sense, the healing of lepers was a miracle. Something happened that only God could do. Someone benefited from it and the public gave the credit to God, which in turn drew them closer to God, affecting his plan.

Other examples of miracles are both spectacular and non-spectacular in variety. For example: the walking of Jesus on the water and calming the storm and sea, the feeding of many thousands with only a few fish and loaves of bread, the raising of Lazarus from the dead, the opening of the Red Sea and millions of people passing across on dry land, and so on and so forth.

These miracles were truly extraordinary events with sensational results. Imagine someone stepping in front of an approaching hurricane and commanding the winds to calm and the clouds to disperse, or imagine a man who had been in the grave for several days standing up and living again because someone uttered the words "come forth."

When we consider the magnitude of these biblical miracles, we find accepting the loose application of the word today very difficult. Today miracle is assigned to someone winning the lottery, an underdog team unexpectedly winning, or, as in our discussion, a departed pet speaking to their people in a dream. I do not see how a person winning the lottery helps anyone but the person actually winning. I do not see too many people rejoicing for someone else who has won their money. I remember hearing of one fellow who had just won his second lottery. He was on television and his comment was, "I sure am glad I won again because the other $3 million I had won a few years ago is almost gone." His comment did nothing to make me feel better. In fact, I felt a little perturbed at the man. His winning did nothing for the public, who undoubtedly felt the same way I did. Furthermore, I did not see how God's plan was advanced or what it might even have been.

The same is true when it comes to our pets. There are no public miracles. We all grieve deeply when we lose them, and certainly God is concerned about that. It breaks God's heart when one of the people he created is broken and grieving. Anytime one of his creatures suffers physical death, it grieves him because it was not at all what he wanted for us. I believe that is one reason why he led me to write my first book, to bring the comforting of his Word to them who would otherwise not know it. But when some claim to have had supernatural experiences where departed pets visit and speak to them, we need to pause and consider what the Bible has to say about this, putting aside personal prejudice or experiences. Only in this way can we differentiate between what is from God and what is not, because there is a lot out there that is definitely *not* of God.

Clearly, these "sightings" and "visions" do not qualify as miracles. They do not meet the criteria of what a miracle is or what it is meant to accomplish. Moreover, with the evidence in the previous chapters, we can safely assume that many of these experiences are not from God at all, and therefore, cannot be trusted. So, let us turn to the next chapter to draw some final conclusions about this topic of miracles.

Chapter 13

THE VERDICT ON MIRACLES

Does God still perform public miracles? What about the stupendous and stunning miracles we see recorded in scripture? No doubt many believe that he does. Why would anyone doubt that? Is he not still God? Does he not still have the power to do them? Well, let me answer those questions with a question. Can you name for me a miracle that God has performed recently on the scale of those we see in scripture?

Name just one—just one extraordinary event that happened during your lifetime that you believe was a true biblical-caliber miracle. Has someone parted a sea recently? Has someone called down fire from the heavens? Has a boy with a basket full of bread and fish fed thousands? If so, I will gladly pay his way to go to places like Somalia to help feed the poor. Has anyone been raised from the dead? Of course, the answer to all of these questions is no because miracles in the true biblical sense and definition no longer happen. And there is good reason for this.

When I gave you the criteria for qualifying an extraordinary event as a miracle, I held back part of the explanation as to why miracles were used. I did so for good reason. I wanted to give you a foundational understanding of *what* constituted a miracle, but I did not want you to confuse that information with *why* miracles were used. The reason why they were used is the same reason why they are no longer used. If that sounds a bit confusing, do not worry, I will clear that up directly. But please know that this is a very important fact about miracles, and you need to grasp it if you are going to have the right perspective in a world gone miracle crazy.

In the Bible, especially in the New Testament, miracles were performed for one primary reason. There were other reasons to be sure, but the most important reason for miracles or, for that matter, signs and wonders was to attest to the authority of the individual who performed them. Without this power, the authority of the individual was called into question. Let me explain. In the New Testament, we are introduced to the twelve Apostles (Paul filling the vacancy left by Judas). These men were no different from you and me at the time of their calling. They were flesh and blood (or should I say calcium and water?), just like the rest of us. They struggled with their faith and had doubts like anyone else. In fact, in the very beginning, their faith was quite anemic and powerless.

They did not do much for the Lord while he was alive with them, but after the Lord's death, they became giants in the faith. All lived consecrated and spiritually powerful lives after the ascension of Christ. God used them as vessels of honor to pen the New Testament and to publish the gospel to the world. They served faithfully, without wavering, even unto their own untimely end. They suffered through great persecution and ridicule. All, with the exception of John, gladly became martyrs for their faith, their legacies forever captured on the very pages on which they wrote. They were boiled in oil, shot with arrows, dragged to death by wild horses, and endured a host of other cruelties in their devotion to the Lord.

Before ultimately being martyred for the Lord, they were given the tremendous responsibility of publishing the gospel to the world and tasked with growing the church. To accomplish their work, they were endowed with great authority and power above and beyond what any Christian possesses today. As the Apostles (and others of the early disciples) carried out the Lord's commission to preach the gospel, they performed miracles such as raising the dead, healing the palsied and sick, casting out demons, and so on. They were flawless in their faith, performing these extraordinary acts at will. Some today would have you believe that they have this power that the Apostles had. They do not. No Christian today can perform a miracle. There are those who will deceive you into thinking they can, but they cannot. The Apostles were empowered with special abilities to perform spectacular miracles at will. The reason the Apostles had these extraordinary powers and others today do not is that they needed to be able to attest to the truth they were preaching.

The Apostles did not have a copy of the Bible as you and I have. In fact, even though these were the men God would use to write most of the twenty-seven books of the New Testament, much of it had not yet been written. They could not point out chapter and verse to the people they spoke with.

Today, just as I am doing here, I can prove the truth of what I am saying about God by pointing to what he says in his Word.

I have the authority of the Bible to attest to the truth I am telling
you. The Apostles were not able to do that. They could not run
to the corner Bible Bookstore and purchase a New Testament to
show the people hearing them that it was so. So God, in his infinite wisdom, endowed them with special powers and authority to
use at their discretion to attest to the truth they were speaking.

And when they used this power, people of their day did exactly what people of our day would do if they saw someone raised
from the dead or demons cast out. They looked at it as a miracle from God attesting to the truth that the men were telling
them. Even those who lived back in those dark days knew that
no man had such power except what was given to him by God.
So if a man could perform such miraculous things, God's authority surely rested on his shoulders. That miracle was a witness from God that the men speaking were speaking for him. We
read in the book of Hebrews 2:4:

> *God also bearing them [Apostles] witness, both with*
> *signs and wonders, and with divers miracles, and*
> *gifts of the Holy Ghost, according to His own will.*

The Apostles would counsel or teach the people in the name
of God. So they would not appear to be as so many other empty
voices that made this claim, God gave them the power to perform mighty acts to attest to or authenticate what they were saying. In so doing, the first few words of the verse assure us that
God was bearing them witness that they were from him.

While this sort of thing was not commonplace, it was not
unknown to the people. In Acts 2:22, the same was said of the

miracles Jesus performed. This had been a long-established requirement for identifying those who truly spoke for God. This
was necessary because there were many imposters in those days
who claimed to be from God but who had no power and no authority, just as there are today.

There are so many who claim to be of God, but who are not.
They usurp God's authority and turn so many from the truth.
How do we know who is of God and who is not? The answer is
so simple that most people miss it. In one of the several books
written by the Apostle John, the book of 1 John 4:1–3, we are told:

> *Beloved, believe not every spirit, but try the spirits*
> *whether they are of God: because many false prophets*
> *are gone out into the world. Hereby know ye the*
> *Spirit of God; every spirit that confesseth that Jesus*
> *Christ is come in the flesh is of God: and every spirit*
> *that confesseth not that Jesus Christ is come in the*
> *flesh is not of God: and this is that spirit of*
> *antichrist, whereof ye have heard that it should come,*
> *and even now already is it in the world.*

God says we are to test the spirits to see whether they are
from him or not. That test is based on their acknowledgment or
rejection of Jesus Christ as the Son of God. If they are not of
him, they are the deceitful spirits of Antichrist. And this is important, God says that "many" false prophets (false voices) are
in the world. The indication is that you have more chances of
running into a deceitful spirit than you do a truthful one.

I submit to you, and not at all out of context with the Apostle John's writings, that to confess Jesus Christ means that one accepts the Bible as the perfect Word of God, for it is here, in this timeless, inspired book that Jesus is revealed to us. It is the record written by the Spirit of truth. Without the written word, we cannot know the truth. One cannot truly believe in the Christ revealed by the Bible if one does not believe the Bible to begin with. Therefore, we can safely conclude that if a person claims to be of God, what they say, what they write, and what they believe must be based on what God has said in his word. It follows then that what they teach must never conflict with any other teaching of the Bible, or they have erred. God is not the author of confusion, and his Word is never in conflict with itself.

You can see why it was important for the Apostles to be so empowered by the Lord. Their listeners could not compare what they were saying to the Word of God to make sure they were telling the truth as you and I are able to do today when someone makes such a claim. They did not have the entire Bible available to them as we do. Belief in what they were hearing came because of the witness of the power the Apostles had from on high. They were doing exactly what the Lord Jesus had commissioned them to do according to the last verse of the last chapter of the Gospel of Mark:

And they went forth, and preached everywhere, the
Lord working with them and confirming the word
with signs following.

As the Apostles went about doing the business God had appointed to them, preaching the gospel of the Lord, the Lord worked with them and through them from above by providing miraculous power to confirm and validate that what they were saying to the people was true and that it was from God. That power included not only doing miraculous things but having wisdom and knowledge of the things of God that they did not previously possess. When God equips someone to do a job, he is thorough.

You might say "Okay, I can see all that, and it makes sense to me, but you said that public miracles have stopped. Why and when did that happen? I just don't get it." Fair enough. Let us address that. I have already hinted that the reason they stopped is the same reason they began, but let me give you a clearer response than that.

In 1 Corinthians 13, we have what is commonly called the Love chapter. In most Bibles the word will appear as "charity," in some "agape," but the meaning is love, Godly love. Here, one of the most prominent attributes of God is discussed in detail, the love of God, which passes all understanding. The Apostle Paul, led by the Spirit of God, delineates the many properties of Godly love in verses 1–8 of 1 Corinthians. I would encourage anyone who thinks they know what love is to do a study of the love of God. It will overwhelm you, I assure you. His love is perfect and flawless. But moving on, Paul caps the description of love in verses 8–10:

> *Charity [love] never faileth: but whether there be prophecies, they shall fail; whether there be tongues, they shall cease; whether there be knowledge, it shall vanish away. For we know in part, and we prophesy*

> *in part. But when that which is perfect is come, then*
> *that which is in part shall be done away.*

Now a lot is being said in these few verses, but what I want you to see are a few things pertinent only to our study. God is saying through Paul that prophecies (teachings), knowledge, and other demonstrable gifts were going to vanish away. In other words, the special gifts that the Apostles had were going to end. They would exist no more. He frames it against the contrasting idea that love will never end, to give his statement substance.

The logical question is, why would they end? There is purpose to everything God does, so what is the purpose in this? In fact, by answering the *why*, I think we can also answer the *when*. Look at verses 9 and 10. Paul is speaking of himself and the other disciples when he admits the following:

> *For we know in part, and we prophesy in part.*
> *But when that which is perfect is come, then that*
> *which is in part shall be done away.*

No doubt, they were teaching all they knew and then some, but there was more to come—something better and more complete than what they had, something that would preclude or supersede the need for what they had, something *perfect*.

Many people believe that this "that which is perfect" is speaking of the second advent or second coming of Jesus Christ because he is the only one who is perfect. I can understand how some can make that conclusion. However, a complete study of these passages will not allow that conclusion. These passages are not speaking of a person, but rather a thing, specifically knowledge and truth.

While Jesus is the perfect truth incarnate, we do not have him here on earth in person so that he can speak truth to us whenever we need it as we serve him. When he returns, we will have truth incarnate again, but it is not at his coming that truth will be needed to complete his great commission to us; it is now. If we are going to publish the gospel, we need the perfect truth now. We need perfect truth now to convince and convict the world of their need for God. Jesus is the Living Word of God incarnate, but the Bible is the Living Word in writing. It is the perfect mind and perfect will of God transmitted to humankind by God himself.

Paul was saying that we will have these gifts of the Holy Spirit to attest to the truth we are speaking because now we only know a small part of the truth, but when that which is perfect comes, we will not need these partial things because we will have the complete and perfect truth to present to the world.

The Word of God or the Bible is the perfect thing he was speaking of. When God used the Apostles to pen the New Testament, that which was in part (the Apostle's individual and collective knowledge) was done away with and that which was perfect (the perfect Word of God) arrived. It alone contains both the partial knowledge the Apostles possessed, plus the rest of what God wanted us to know.

No longer do disciples of the Lord need to show that we speak for him by miraculous signs and wonders. All we need to do is open the Bible and people can see for themselves what the Almighty has said. The authority and power once used to do the miraculous is now embodied in the perfect Word of God. The words that record God's mind and will toward man have supernatural authority and influence upon the reader. They are like the words of no other book. The Bible claims for itself this authority in Hebrews 4:12:

> For the word of God is quick [alive] and powerful,
> and sharper than any two-edged sword, piercing
> even to the dividing asunder of soul and spirit and
> of the joint and marrow and is a discerner of the
> thoughts and intent of the heart.

The Bible speaks to each reader on an individual basis, knowing the thoughts and heart of the individual turning its pages. One passage can say one thing to a reader and something completely different, yet appropriate, to another. Whatever it says to the reader will be personalized to reach into that individual's essence and stir his or her soul. What other book can claim the perfection and power of the Bible?

No other theory fits, no other hypothesis is acceptable. The inspired word of God is "that which is perfect." And since that which is perfect has come, then that which was in part has been done away with. This included the at-will gifts available to the followers of the Lord during pre-Bible times.

Miracles, signs, and wonders were unquestionably in place to attest to the truth of God being taught by the early disciples and Apostles. These miracles were definable by the standards we set earlier: they were public, were extraordinary, benefited humankind, and brought glory to God. Somehow, somewhere along the line in history, humankind got the notion that anything strange or unexplainable qualified as a miracle. Before we understood how the body worked, if a man had lifted an enormous boulder from off the leg of a loved one, the ability to lift was not the adrenaline that gave him the strength but a miracle. A little further on in history, superstition was sprinkled into the equation, and the scope of what qualified as a miracle was broadened to include the most ridiculous.

Extraordinary things do happen, but ordinary people who do extraordinary things cause them. The 1980 U.S. Olympic Hockey Team victory was not a miracle. Had the sky opened up and a giant stick slapped the puck in, maybe. But that is not what happened. What happened was a group of ordinary individuals came together in an extraordinary way and accomplished an extraordinary feat. There was nothing miraculous about it. Miracles are no more. They are no longer needed.

Now then, make no mistake, according to God, there are some huge miracles coming in the future. There will be all sorts of things happening during the final 1,007 years of this earth, including odd creatures coming out of the earth to attack men, an enormous star named Wormwood hitting the earth, and a city sitting in the clouds, just to name a few. But those miraculous events will be confined to special periods of time that God has blocked off for the end times, periods called the Tribulation and Millennium. During the final time, public miracles just will not happen. I did not say that people would not claim they happened, just that they will not happen. I know that this does not sit well with a lot of folks who love the hype and sensationalism associated with their religious beliefs, but I have no alternative but to state with emphasis what the Bible teaches on this topic.

Again, people love the sensational and just because miracles have ceased is no reason to think the hype will. Pseudomiraculous events are reported all the time. For instance, some of you who live in the northeast may remember that Easter Sunday back in the mid-1960s, when one of the strongest weather fronts on record moved through northern New Jersey, New York, and much of New England. I lived in New Jersey at the time and I remember it like it was yesterday. It was partly cloudy and cool. A front moved across the region in the midafternoon. It grew as dark as I think I have ever seen the sky get during daylight hours. I have to be honest with you, it was definitely a little spooky and a bit like that scene in *The Ten Commandments* movie in which Moses stood on the rock and the clouds gathered.

It grew so dark so quickly that it got everyone's attention right up to the White House. It is virtually a forgotten event now, but back then the story dominated the news for the next few weeks as people of meteorology and religion analyzed the event. No doubt the fact that it happened on Easter Sunday only added to the hype. Rumors started circulating that it had been a miracle or some sort of a "warning from God." Someone even suggested that aliens were behind it. Eyewitnesses were interviewed in great numbers and the hype continued. It eventually fizzled out, of course. But my point is that even though it was obviously a naturally occurring weather front, educated and professional people just could not help sensationalizing and hyping it up.

It was just a weather front. No one rose from the dead, the

lame did not walk, and the blind did not suddenly see. No miraculous event was associated with it, no alien spacecraft landed, and no judgment came for whatever we were supposedly being warned about. Yet, people rushed to hype it up. We love the unexplainable. Worse, we love to explain the unexplainable in sensational ways. But in fact all that happened was that it got really dark for a few minutes and then it passed.

As of 2010, I had been living in Kansas for several years. I can tell you with conviction that the weather here is routinely sensational. In fact, during the spring and summer you can expect severe weather on a weekly basis. It did not take long for us to experience it; my wife and I were exposed to our first sensational Kansas weather experience within five days of arriving in Topeka. We happened to be at the local grocery store. When we entered the store at 2 P.M., it was sunny and bright, with a wisp of summer wind. At checkout, a mere thirty minutes later, it was so dark outside that you could not see the cars in the parking lot, except for those that had their lights on. A storm had moved in so quickly from beyond the horizon that it had caught the whole city off guard. The skies were black, lightning was crashing, and the wind was actually pushing heavy shopping carts uphill.

I was of the misconception that Kansas was supposed to be dry and dusty. It was far from it that day. The rain was unbelievable. Raised in Hawaii, I had seen monsoon-type weather many times before, but this was beyond that. The heavy rain was being driven by seventy miles per hour winds and was peppered with hail the size of nickels. It rained two inches in thirty minutes and nine hundred lightning strikes were registered in less than one hour (I learned later that Topeka held the world's record in lightning strikes as if that was something to keep track of and gloat about).

Half the city lost power and there was debris everywhere. The runoff canals that were previously dry and tranquil were now rushing torrents of water. Needless to say, we questioned our decision to move to Topeka. And lest anyone believe this was an isolated occurrence, just last year we experienced a day darker than even that Easter Sunday so many years ago. The sky darkened to near midnight status. Things were only visible during the many, many lightning strikes. And then the hail came and came and came. I held hail in my hand larger than a softball. The news reported one hailstone nearly seven inches in diameter.

Not one vehicle of the 1,500 automobiles parked in this area had a windshield or back window when the storm passed. My truck was destroyed, and while it was only thirty feet away from where I was in the building, I could not see but only hear the destruction taking place because of the darkness. Now irrespective of the fact that the media once again assigned a supernatural flavor to this event and questioned what we had done to deserve such a calamity, neither this nor the other two events I mentioned in the preceding were miraculous in any sense of the word. They were just extraordinary weather-related experiences that superstition helped hype to a supernatural level.

So there you have the Bible take on public miracles, signs, and wonders. The final verdict is that they just no longer occur for the reasons I have carefully cited. They are no longer needed. They no longer would serve the purpose they once served. That purpose is being fulfilled by the Bible, which is itself a miraculous book.

Often truth can be offensive or can come across as negative. I hope that is not the case here. I mean to foster a positive understanding of this phenomenon we are exploring. I understand that many, many pet people are experiencing the unexplainable, and I have done my best to offset some of the baseless, New Age misinformation people are exposed to, with solid, dependable scripture. With that accomplished, I now need to provide the uplifting, encouraging analysis that I promised you. I am sorry to have rained on the public miracle parade, but I think you will find what follows in the next chapter very comforting and exciting.

Chapter 14

GODLY COMFORT

When we label something a miracle, we assign a public application to it. The public was meant to witness miracles. In my opinion, these ghost pet experiences that many report are not meant for public consumption but rather are exclusively for the person(s) God is dealing with in order to comfort them. I suppose it would not be technically wrong to refer to these experiences as private miracles, but a better definition might be "private comforting." That has a more personal, intimate tone for me, and when I am down and looking to God for comfort, I need to know that he is concerned about me and that in this world of nearly seven billion souls he has his eye upon me and knows what I need in my life.

Previously, we saw convincing evidence that proved that God would not allow people or animals to return to this life once they have passed on. We saw that despite even the best reasons we might imagine he should do this, God simply does not allow it. God never acts in conflict with his own Word, and scripture does not provide for this eventuality. In fact, we identified several passages and incidents where interacting with those who had passed on was clearly forbidden. There can be no doubt that it was, is, and will always be disallowed by God. He simply does not allow the dead to return or otherwise contact the living.

On the other hand, we must acknowledge that there are occasions when people do have these supernatural experiences. So we are clear, I acknowledge that they are supernatural. In the majority of the cases, they can be nothing else. Something is going on. A lot of good, dependable people are seeing and hearing things that cannot be explained. Some are having vivid, often recurring dreams that seem so real. So somehow, we have to reconcile the fact that God does not allow those who have passed on to contact us with the experiences we are having so that they make sense.

The only scenario that fits and satisfies both camps of thought is that God the Father is personally dealing with his children on an individual basis. If you take the position that God is performing public miracles, your argument will fail. If you take the position that animals and people have the ability to reach back from beyond the grave to contact us, your argument will fail. The only possible position that is supported by a preponderance of scriptural evidence is that God reaches out to his children in unique and customized ways that only they can relate to and understand.

Later in this chapter, I will share with you a true account of how God used a private comforting in my life to help me and how he made sure I knew it could only have come from him. God always works on an individual basis in these situations, and the way he touched my life was quite moving. More importantly, it was tailor-made for me. What he did would not have meant anything to anyone else in the world. I am sure you will enjoy reading the account.

The point that I want to drive home is that it was a private thing, not a miracle. God was just reaching down and touching a believer in a way that was unmistakably supernatural. It was between him and me. That I later decided to publicize the experience to help others did not make it a miracle. It remains a private comforting that was made public only so others could glean hope and faith from it as I pray you will in a few moments. That is all. Nothing miraculous to it at all as you shall see.

As a point of interest, in my particular experience there was also a public or social element to it. While it was private in the sense that God was comforting me in my time of need, he was also preparing me to be able to empathize with others who would contact me in the future with similar experiences. Since that time he has led me to publish many books and articles on this topic and moved tens of thousands of people to contact me to discuss their personal losses and experiences. People often thank me for the many hours of time and help I give them, and their expressions of appreciation are always endearing. But the truth is, it is I who am thankful. I am thankful that God has used me to help, that he has given me the knowledge to be able to help, and that people place confidence in that help. I cannot possibly explain how humbling all of that is.

I apologize for the rabbit trail. Moving on, there should not be a lot of fanfare and hype when God provides private comforting in someone's life. If he does it privately, I think his intent to keep the comforting private should be honored. On the other hand, that does not mean that we cannot publicly acknowledge that he has done something marvelous in our lives in order to give him the much-deserved credit. We should be quick to give him praise and credit for those things. But it should remain a private matter in our hearts.

Now before we get to my story, there are a couple of others I would like to share. We are discussing pet-related experiences, but I did not want to give the impression that receiving comfort from God is limited just to grief-stricken pet people. Indeed, he can and does touch the lives of whomever he will. This adds credence to what I have been saying.

Throughout time God has worked on a personal level with those who love and trust him. Let me give you several examples of what I am talking about. With the exception of the second example, I know all the following accounts I am going to share with you to be true.

EXAMPLE 1

The wife of my pastor from many years ago was diagnosed with several bleeding ulcers. She was in quite serious condition with great pain. The prognosis was not at all good without surgery, but the required surgery was complicated and quite risky. It was also quite expensive. She suffered greatly from this ailment, but opted to put the surgery on the back burner while she appealed more strongly to the Lord to intervene.

Through much prayer from the entire congregation, and several other churches, in just three short weeks her ulcers had completely disappeared. Now you can claim that the X-rays were smudged and there never were any ulcers, that the diagnosis was flawed, or that the doctor erred in his original diagnosis. I suppose those things are possible, but not likely. I was there. I witnessed the excruciating pain that she endured, and I also saw it wane and disappear. You will never convince me that God did not inject himself into the equation for one of his children. He healed that woman because she trusted in him. God intervenes in the lives of his children. He heals their hearts and their bodies.

EXAMPLE 2

The pastor of a large midwestern church, a man I have admired and tried to emulate all of my Christian life, relays a story in one of his published books about a service where he had preached a very strong message on the need for people to receive Jesus Christ as their personal savior.

He said that a woman of Asian descent made her way up to the front of the church after the sermon and began speaking to him in Chinese. The pastor tried to stop her, explaining he could not speak Chinese, but she did not understand him as she could not speak English. Eventually, a relative who was with her and could speak both languages came to their rescue. He relayed what she wanted to say to the preacher. In streaming tears, she told her relative that she had done exactly what the preacher had told her to do. She had bowed her head and asked forgiveness in the name of Jesus Christ.

She had heard the message in Chinese. How is that possible? This man did not know one word of Chinese. He had preached in English. She did not understand English. Is this bizarre? Perhaps. But I think it is just God working in that individual way we just spoke of. For me, that situation was not bizarre at all as I had a similar experience myself. Had I not been there, had it not happened to me, I would never have believed it. That account follows.

EXAMPLE 3

As a volunteer prison chaplain in Dade and Broward County, Florida, in the 1980s, I was regularly scheduled to speak to groups of maximum security inmates in a Broward County facility. Because of the heavy population of Hispanic men in this facility, it was reasonable to assume that there would be a significant percentage of men present who spoke only Spanish. To ensure that their needs were met, the Spanish pastor from my church, a good friend of mine and fellow Miami Dolphin fan, agreed to interpret for me as I spoke.

Unfortunately, when the time came for me to speak, the Spanish pastor had not yet arrived. Due to the threat level of these particular inmates and the increase in gang-related assaults, variances from schedules were not allowed. Consequently, we could not delay the service and wait for my interpreter to arrive.

Reluctantly, I forged ahead and brought what I considered a very strong and challenging salvation message. I was a little concerned by the thought that some of the twenty-seven men in attendance would not be able to understand what I was saying, but I struggled against letting that hamper my delivery. Nevertheless, I made a special effort to speak slowly and to articulate my words as clearly as possible, in the hope that anyone who understood a little English might pick up some of what I was saying.

I was experienced enough with speaking to large crowds so that I knew they were getting it. There were no yawns, no glassed-over eyes, no glances at the clock on the wall. Each of the attendees seemed genuinely interested in what I was saying. For that reason, somewhere in the middle of my sermon I just assumed they all understood English, and I felt comfortable picking up the tempo so I would not go into overtime.

After the message, I invited the men to come forward for prayer or for more assistance or counseling. Without any urging, three gentlemen stood up and made their way to the front of the room. I could see that they had tears in their eyes and sensed the urgency of their need to talk to someone. At just about the same moment, the Spanish pastor came rushing in, quietly apologizing to me for being late. He had been caught in traffic, something you never need to apologize for in Miami.

I asked him please to help the men coming forward and to deal with whatever issues were bothering them as I closed the service. He graciously consented to do so. Perhaps fifteen minutes later, he came to me with a puzzled look and said, "I didn't know you spoke Spanish?"

I said, "Well, I don't really—just a few words."

He looked very surprised, almost startled. Then he shared

with me that the three men who came forward, and perhaps half of the other men who were in attendance, did not speak any English at all. I asked, "Well what did the men come forward for?"

He said, "They heard the gospel message in Spanish as you preached and wanted to accept Jesus."

For some reason, what he told me did not surprise me as much as you might think, but it did stir me. Outside I accepted without any fanfare what my friend told me, acknowledging it with a simple wonderful. Inside, however, I was quietly thinking, Wow, Lord, wow . . . how cool is that? because I knew even though I am not capable of doing something miraculous like that, he is. But he does so privately without much fanfare, and so I wanted to keep it in my heart rather than celebrating it out loud.

EXAMPLE 4

I have met perhaps one thousand missionaries since becoming a Christian back in 1974. Each of them are heroes to me: courageous and unselfish folks who leave the safe confines of our wonderful country to follow the will of God to live on foreign shores where neither their freedom nor well-being are ensured.

They often do without even the most basic of luxuries that we enjoy back here at home like soap, milk, and the Internet. Some have had to send their children to school hundreds of miles from where they were living because there was no local school system. They often will not see their young children for many weeks at a time. Others have contracted awful diseases or been assaulted or slain at the hands of those they went to serve. Some have had to bury their children during their service there. It is a very difficult life in many ways, to be sure. But I have never heard one missionary or their family members complain about what the Lord required of them. In fact, just the opposite is true. Often, in the face of great adversity, their burdens are masked behind warm and enthusiastic smiles. Where one would expect bitterness, they have a spirit of joy.

At face value, they appear to have subjected themselves to a life of misery for their faith. The truth is that they are genuinely and sincerely happy in their respective fields of service. For them, not to have gone to the mission field would have meant a life of discontent. No misery is worse than struggling against the call of God. They would have been unfulfilled and out of place anywhere but where they were supposed to be. For missionaries, God places a people upon their hearts and there is no alternative but to go and serve.

I have heard account after account of seemingly miraculous events from the ranks of these heroes of the faith. Of course, they are not miracles at all, but rather, private interventions. There are so many to choose from, but I have selected just one to serve as our fourth example. I will not mention names, but some of you will know of whom I speak when you read this account.

A new missionary had arrived on the field with his wife and two children. They heard what difficulty their predecessors had experienced with the indigenous peoples and were eager to get to work and try their hand at winning their hearts. Despite warnings that the natives were historically hostile to outsiders, the missionary proposed that he and his family should go into the jungle together and make first contact as quickly as they could.

Having already learned much of the language before their arrival, they felt they could easily converse with tribal leadership and successfully communicate why they had come.

To their dismay however, they were not well received. The fact that they had learned the language and could talk without interpreters gave them no advantage. They were not wanted. In fact, they were told to leave the jungle and not return. The missionary told the chief that they would not leave, that they could not leave, because they needed to tell his people about the true God who had sent them there. The chief angrily told the missionary that he did not care for anything he had to offer and that they needed to leave the jungle immediately. If they did not, he and his family would be slain.

The chief made a gesture to some other natives and soon drums began beating. The chief, growing increasingly more agitated, raised his voice and told the missionary to leave. He warned that when the drums stopped beating, the warriors would come and slay his family. I am ashamed to say that I would have been on the first canoe out of there. My paddling would have been reminiscent of a cartoon as I rapidly dipped the oar into the water and my canoe lifted out of the water. But then I am not made of the stuff God makes missionaries out of.

But this dear man of God, his wife, and children did not get into their canoe. They had no intention of leaving. Instead, they went back to the thatched hut, where they had left their camping gear. This was a hut other unsuccessful missionaries had built years before. Once inside, the missionary called a family meeting and unanimously decided that they were there because it was where God wanted them to be, and therefore, they were there to stay. They joined hands as a family and fell on their faces in prayer.

Of course, they prayed for their own safety, but their real plea was that the hearts of the natives might be softened so that they might do the work God wanted them to do. Throughout the night and the beating of the drums, they prayed. I can only imagine the anguish that each of them felt as they earnestly uttered their petitions. No doubt, their minds wandered to thoughts of their safe home back in America and of their friends and family. A part of them longed to be there. Thoughts of the hatred the natives felt for them and the sound of those terrifying drums surely weighed heavily upon them as well.

No one could blame them if they gave up and left. No one expected them to die in the jungle. There was no need for that. That would be absurd. No doubt they thought about fleeing for their lives. But they did not. They remained together in prayer, a family surrendered to the Lord's will, and waited to see what the chief would do. After hours of praying, the drums suddenly stopped. There was nothing but silence. The temptation to end their prayers and run came again, but they did not falter. They remained in prayer. Then the missionary paused in his prayer for a moment, looked up, and listened intently. He thought he had heard footsteps, but he was not sure. When his children looked up, he beckoned them to bow there heads again and they continued in prayer. An hour passed and then two hours. Finally, the rays of the morning sun were starting to filter through the poorly thatched hut. They rose from prayer and looked outside. There were no warriors. There was no trouble. The missionary told his wife and children to wait while he went to the village. Mustering supernatural courage, he headed off into the jungle. When he arrived at the village, the chief came running up to him with a big smile on his face. In his native tongue he said, "We will now hear of this God you speak of."

The missionary, thinking perhaps the threat had actually been a practical joke of some sort or a test of courage from the chief and not a real threat, said, "So you really didn't mean to hurt us?"

The chief said, "No, when I stop drums, I tell warriors go to kill all. But we could not attack your hut because of all your warriors."

The missionary said, "Warriors? I had no warriors."

"Oh, yes," the chief said, "many warriors, warriors of flame, all around hut, on top hut, on path, in jungle. . . . You have much power. . . . Your God is strong God. We want this God."

The chief's words made the missionary realize that God had supernaturally intervened for his family and him during the night. He was temporarily overwhelmed by emotion as I am simply from typing the account for you. Tears of joy ran down his cheeks. The chief's story was extraordinary, but he knew that the chief was telling the truth. He realized that God had heard and answered their prayers. God rewards faith and the right attitude.

This missionary and his family were blessed of God in a very real and personal way. Their lives were at risk, and in faith, they waited upon the Lord and trusted his providence. And once the Lord acted, they did not view it as a miracle, in the sense that it brought public attention to God. Rather, they saw it as the loving care of a Father for his children. It was a private matter for them, one they would only share when it would bring appropri-

ate glory to God, but never with fanfare. The work that was accomplished with those indigenous people would never have been
realized if it were not for God intervening and providing grace
and protection. Some would look for a way to explain this whole
story away, but that would be a waste of their time. There is no
denying that God was at work here.

In each of the examples I have given you, God did something
extraordinary either for his children or through his children to
accomplish his purposes. And he did it in a private way without
a lot of hoopla and hype. That is the way he does things today.
He does not perform (or have someone else perform) miracles in
public because that no longer serves his purposes.

You may believe this story or not. That is your choice. For
those who understand how God works in today's world, it may
not be a typical experience, but it is very believable. God is always touching our lives in some wonderful way, but it is done
so on a private and personal level, as a Father to his children. He
helps in our lives in tangible ways, from paving the way for our
success to posting guardian, or rather guarding, angels around
us to comfort us during our failures or losses.

When it comes to the loss of a pet, God cares about our pain
and our grief. He knows what we are going through because Jesus
suffered through pain and grief so that he might be the perfect
Lord, understanding the infirmities and weaknesses of our flesh.
So when God comforts his child or speaks to his or her heart, he
does so because he indeed feels our pain.

In my case, God spoke to me in a very certain way, a way that
I would never have imagined and a way no one else would understand. It was very private and I told only my wife about it.

Later on I shared it with readers who were experiencing great difficulty dealing with their grief because I knew it would help them. Finally, I offer it now publicly because I think it gives credence to what I am trying to convey to you about some of the ways God deals with his children.

My experience actually took place in my office at work, but for you to understand the significance of what happened, I am going to have to give you some background information. In 1996 I lost my beloved Samantha, a fifteen-year-old West Highland white terrier. As you might expect, I was feeling very, very down and depressed.

Her passing came very unexpectedly. She had what appeared to be a cold and so my wife ran her to the veterinarian that day. The veterinarian said he wanted to keep her for the night, and in the morning he phoned to tell us that she had passed away, that her heart had given out. I was devastated. Sam had been my shadow for so many years, and she had been so totally devoted to me. How could I have left her away from home that night? I felt that I had let her down. She went everywhere I went. I never had to look for her or call to her. She was always near me. For her to pass away without me by her side made me feel as if I had failed her when she had never failed me. Like many of you, I found out the hard way that she was more important to me than I had realized. I found out too late how much she meant to me. Not being able to communicate that to her ate me up inside. In fact, other memories of my failures with her began to haunt me and caused me to feel great guilt.

The previous month we had been on a trip to Florida. I'd parked and stepped out of the van to stretch and as I was stretching, I noticed this little log going over a muddy, boggy area at the side of the road. The log led to a little island full of flowers and bushes. Being a nature lover, I couldn't resist taking a closer look, so I walked across the log and did a little exploring in the meadow on the other side of this bog. I then walked through some tall bushes that led away from the bog and eventually came back to the van without having to pass over the log again. I suppose, in retrospect, it actually wasn't an island at all.

Unknown to me, Sam had jumped out of the van for a stretch too. She had seen me go across the log. Shadow that she was, she wanted to follow, but being afraid of heights, she opted to forego the log and transit the mud it spanned instead. I noticed her movement just before she stepped into the bog and I yelled "*Sam, no Sam.*" Unfortunately, she kept on going. The years had taken a toll on her hearing. She had heard me. I could tell by her ears going up when I yelled to her. But she could not tell where my voice was coming from. So, upon hearing me yell her name, her ears popped up and she headed in the direction she had remembered seeing me go. She dove right into that nasty, smelly bog. I am sure you know what I mean by bog. It is that awful smelling claylike slosh that you usually find in stagnant water with rotting vegetation. Her white fur was all black and smelly. She had managed to get herself covered with that muck from head to toe in less time than it took me to run the fifteen feet to pull her out.

I was so upset at her that I yelled at her, and when I found a hose on a nearby building, I gave her a really rough bath (which by the way did not help the smell at all). I scolded her and scrubbed her, and the little trooper just stood there and took it, happy to be with her daddy no matter what. All I could think of when the veterinarian told me that she was gone was how angry I had gotten with her for being so faithful. I had treated her like a queen all her life, but all I could remember was that one heartless moment. It grieved me very deeply. Many of you will understand that I would have done anything for just two more minutes to smother her in love and to tell her I was sorry for being angry. But it was not to be. It was so devastating.

Let me return to the story. I was in my office. There I was— a grown man, a military officer, a black belt in Karate, a person who used to tag alligators in Florida, a tough guy—just sitting at my desk at work fighting back tears. I wanted to grieve and I wanted to weep uncontrollably, but I had neither the time nor opportunity. Even so, every hour or so I would temporarily lose the battle, shut and lock my office door, and let some tears drop. I think every reader understands what I was going through. These are the moments we all must endure as we wait on time to help heal us.

To continue, on one of the occasions where I felt I needed to close my door that day, I wept out softly, *"Lord, please help me already. I simply cannot take any more."* I was not blaming God for anything. Samantha had lived a good life, a long life. I was her best buddy, and even though I felt bad about the episode at the bog, I knew that she knew I loved her dearly. God had allowed a long friendship. I appreciated that and was not expressing anger. But I was hurting badly and I needed some relief quick. There were moments when I thought I would lose my mind, or perhaps I already had. So I breathed out a prayer. It was a short prayer, a simple prayer, but it captured my desperate state of mind. People sometimes think prayers need to be long-winded and wordy, articulated to perfection. I have found that the spontaneous emptying of one's heart before the Lord receives the best results. And God answered my prayer almost immediately as I sat at my desk. Wait. Let me put you on hold right here for another moment while I fill you in on some needed background detail to ensure that you get the whole impact of my experience.

Throughout my childhood, my father was a navy chief, a submariner. Submariners, as I pointed out in my first book, are a close-knit subculture (no pun intended) of the navy. They stick together and are like one big family.

The navy purposely keeps submariners together. This circumstance is not so on surface ships or shore stations. When you are transferred from one of those units, you seldom see the people you knew there again in your career, but not so with the submarine fleet. Submariners are often reassigned and transferred together. Many times the boat (submarines are called boats, not ships) would receive orders instead of the sailors. So instead of individuals departing the unit and heading in different directions, the unit would be sent to another port, and all the crew members and their families would follow. Consequently, many families would remain friends and neighbors for long periods of time. Such was the case with my father and another shipmate named Tom. We were stationed together in Virginia, Florida, California, and Hawaii over a period of perhaps a dozen years.

I grew up with Tom's kids. His son, Tom Jr., and daughter, Mae, had been my good friends throughout our early years. Mae and I became close friends and shared much. In fact, Mae was the first person ever to try to tell me about the Lord Jesus. That occurred in Honolulu, in the mid-1960s. At that time I declined. I was young and had plans. I wanted nothing to interfere with my life, and just knew that God would mess it up if I let him into it. It would be many years before I realized the folly of such a mindset, but luckily I did.

I lost contact with Tom Jr. and Mae as we grew older and went our separate ways. I married and joined the navy, Tom joined the air force, and Mae joined the army and married (and divorced). We probably crossed paths many times in Honolulu as we were all stationed there at various times, but it was almost a decade later before we would meet up again.

I know I am dragging this out, but the complexities of the story should be interesting. In 1974, I had received the Lord as my savior and became an ardent student of the Bible. In 1976, I was serving on the staff of the commander in chief, U.S. Pacific Fleet, at Pearl Harbor. While being briefed on some newly assigned classified duties, the man mentoring me showed me some family pictures from his wallet (always a joy, right!). He said, "Here is one—real sad, my son was supposed to marry this girl, but the wedding has been called off because she is dying of cancer."

When he handed me the photograph, I was prepared to take a cursory look and offer condolences. Instead, I was overwhelmed to see that his son's intended was Mae! I explained to this man that I had known his son's fiancée her entire life and was devastated by the news. He told me where she was living in Honolulu, and I decided to call her and see if my wife and I could help in any way. I knew I could not call her direct but would have to locate her mother first at work. That may sound odd, but her mother had established a "code" system for the telephone when Mae and her brother were young to protect them from potentially dangerous callers who might find out they were home alone. It was a little different, but that was the way things were.

I was sure that the same code would be in place, but because it had been so many years since I last used it, I could not recall how it went. Fortunately, I did remember where her mother worked and called her. She was so happy to hear from me. We talked and she gave me the code, which was a ring, hang up, ring, hang up, ring again series. I called and Mae answered.

Mae was quite surprised to hear from me and seemed very upbeat. Even though my fellow employee had told me that she was dying, she did not sound like she was at all. Moreover, Mae told me that her cancer was not all that bad, and that it was not a burden to her. So instead of talking about that, we just talked about all that had happened over the years. She was so happy to hear that I had finally accepted the Lord and that my wife and children had also. I knew she would be since she had made such an effort to help me earlier in our lives.

My wife was happy to hear she was better than we had heard and suggested that we call and invite her out to our church. Mae accepted the invitation, and we made plans to pick her up the following Sunday. We were all so excited. Then, the day before we were to pick her up, her mother telephoned to tell me that Mae had passed away the previous evening. I was shocked and very saddened. I realized then that Mae had not wanted me to know what bad shape she actually was in. It was a very sad turn of events. Instead of taking her to church, I was to be a pallbearer at her funeral

I realize that this story is sad, but it is important that you hear it in order to understand what I am now going to say. Returning to the scene in my office again, I was pleading to God for some relief from my pain. I was so far down that I had to look up to see bottom. I did not think that anything could help me, but I forced myself to pray anyway.

All of a sudden, my office was flooded with the fragrance of perfume. Not just any perfume, but a specific perfume that I knew very well. That perfume was Mae's. I'd never known anyone, anywhere, other than Mae who used it. It was a special perfume from Japan that Mae's mother bought her. It wasn't anything special financially speaking; it was just unique and possessed an unmistakable and memorable fragrance. As I said, I have never encountered this perfume, or any that closely resembled it, anywhere else at any time in my life, and especially not in the middle of Kansas. But here it was filling my office with that unmistakable fragrance.

At the very moment I smelled it, I recognized the fragrance. And at that very moment a thought came into my head. Actually, it was not as if the thought came into my head the way thoughts often do. Rather, it was more like hearing a voice inside. Of course, it was not a voice, but it might as well have been. It certainly was not my thought because it came out of nowhere and surprised me.

Very simply I was impressed with the words Samantha is okay. She is here with Mae. Don't worry. At the same moment that I thought I heard She is here with Mae, the fragrance of that unique perfume filled my office. Was it Mae's voice? No, it was not. It

was not even a voice. It was just a thought. Besides, remember
those who have left cannot contact us. Was it Mae's perfume?
Yes, it was. There is no doubt in my mind. I cannot explain it
any better than I already have. I knew, without a doubt that God
had sent this thought to me, accompanied by the fragrance, to
comfort me.

The reason was clear to me. I wanted to know if my Samantha was in heaven. Mae was a close friend I knew to be in heaven
by virtue of her testimony. God would not allow her or anyone
to contact me, but there is no prohibition on him speaking to my
heart. In my wildest dreams, I would not have anticipated that
God could touch me in such a way. Mae had passed away over
twenty years earlier, and I seldom thought about her, if ever.
Certainly, I had not thought of that perfume since last I smelled
it back in the 1960s. And even if I had, I would have never tied
the perfume to my Samantha.

This was my Father enveloping me in his comfort and peace.
He used circumstances that meant nothing in and of themselves,
but he tied them together to speak to me from within and to assure me that he was in control and Samantha was just fine. The
message was private. No one else could have received this message but me. No one else could have understood it. But I did.

For those who are skeptical, know that my office has a glass
panel that faces the only hallway leading to it. No one had passed
by. I would have seen them as I always did. I even opened the
door immediately after smelling the perfume (because even I had
trouble believing it), and no one was around. There was no perfume fragrance in the hall, in the next room, or in any other

room. Moreover, when I returned to my office twenty seconds later, the fragrance was gone from there as well. But as a last gesture, God impressed me with another thought, Don't lose hold of this. I have not.

No doubt some of you will scoff. Others of you will call me a religious fanatic. That is fine. However, you will search near and far to find anyone more fundamental than I when it comes to strict Bible doctrine. I will never buy into the touchy-feely religion of sensationalism or any of the nonsense New Wave Christianity is selling, but I know that God speaks to his people in their hearts. I am not suggesting that God gives extra revelation. I absolutely refute that notion. God has given us his complete word and there is no more to come. But he does speak to his people in their hearts in private. He spoke to me. I know that it was my Lord. He often speaks to me (and all his children) in their hearts. In John 10:27 the Lord said:

My sheep hear my voice.

If you look in the Old Testament book of 1 Kings 19, you will see the account of Elijah, a great prophet of the Lord hiding out in the wilderness in a cave, sulking if you will. I will not recount the entire story, but the Lord causes a great wind to pass by, so strong in fact, that it broke the rocks. And the Word of God says, "But the Lord was not in the wind." Then he caused a great earthquake, but again the Bible says, "But the Lord was not in the earthquake." Then there was a great fire, but again God's Word says, "But the Lord was not in the fire." Finally, the account says, "And after the fire a still small voice."

God could have impressed Elijah with the wind, for it was a formidable wind. It was so strong that it broke rocks. But he did not. He could have impressed Elijah with the earthquake or fire, each a spectacular display of power. But again, he did not. Instead, he spoke to Elijah in a still small voice. He quietly and tenderly comforted his prophet and made things right for him without a lot of fanfare and pomp. That same God who quietly spoke to the heart of Elijah several thousand years ago in the Holy Land spoke gently and softly to my heart in Kansas. That small voice comforted Elijah and it also brought me great comfort and made things right.

For those of you who have had a spiritual or supernatural experience of the type I have described, or perhaps a very vivid dream concerning a departed pet, I hope I have given you the understanding needed to frame your experience correctly. Never forget that there are opposing forces at work around us and that not every spirit is of God. Those forces not only have the motive and opportunity to deceive but have the power to do so as well and they employ that deception whenever there is opportunity. On the other hand, there are occasions when God speaks to our hearts. If God is trying to provide you comfort and you are sure it is he, be careful to show him the appropriate praise and appreciation.

My real goal in this chapter, even this very book, is to keep people from putting too much emphasis on any experience or dream they may have had. I do not doubt the accounts, only the origin and purpose of them. If God is speaking to you, he will because you are his child and he desires to comfort you. He does speak to his children in a very private and personal way, a way that probably is custom made for each one as was my experience. If you are not a child of God, in the sense of being born again as John 3 of God's Word directs, then any experience you have had should be suspect. I urge you to contact me if you have any problems or questions in this regard.

I would like to end with this disclaimer. Please do not think that by becoming a child of God, you will then have one of the experiences I have been discussing. That will not happen. God meets with people when their motives are pure, and my experience has been that he only reaches down in such a way when a real need exists. If you come to God seeking his forgiveness, it must be with a contrite and repenting spirit. There can be no ulterior motive. He will know your heart, whether it is true or not, and he will deal with you one on one as only he can.

Chapter 15

THE SUM OF IT

While there is obviously a prominent theme to this book, my hope is that you also gleaned a lot of peripheral information that will prove helpful to you and answer the questions we all ask about our animals. For people who love and keep pets, people like you and me, we must know the answers to these types of questions and to be secure in the knowledge that we gain by asking them. When we love an animal and take on the responsibility for its life's care, we are in it for the long haul. Our concern for our best friend does not end with its passing. We care about things beyond this life and feel a sense of unrest until we know what eternity holds for them.

I have tried to shed as much light on this subject as I could. Scripture is not silent on this issue, but neither is there an abundance of information to be found in the Bible. I have drawn logical and reasonable conclusions about the afterlife for animals based on what scripture says. Where needed, I speculated and tried to fill in the blanks. I hope the careful and reverent blend of facts and ideas has been uplifting and helpful.

Rather than end with the standard summary of all that has been said as most authors do in the final chapter of their work, I would like to close in my penultimate chapter with what I consider an important message for my fellow pet lovers. I have learned much from my own experiences and those of literally tens of thousands of readers over the years. I am happy to pass along the words of wisdom that they have shared with me in hope that you will benefit from them. Invariably, one of the most expedient reasons that people contact me is to express how stunned they are at the intensity of their grief and pain after the passing of the family pet. They want to know why they feel as bad as they do, and they want help dealing with the despair they are experiencing. They are no different from you or me. We have had to face down that pain ourselves many times.

The condition we find ourselves in when we lose a best friend is overwhelmingly painful. We knew we would have to bid farewell to our beloved pet one day and that it would be painful, but we thought we had prepared ourselves for it mentally and emotionally. That day eventually came, and it brought with it an unexpected depth of darkness and emptiness that we could never have anticipated. In our wildest dreams, we could not have imagined that the emotion of grief could be so deep and consuming.

We find ourselves unable to sleep and unwilling to eat. For many of us, going to work is out of the question, for we are an emotional mess. We cannot concentrate or function and weep at the most inappropriate and inconvenient times. Sweet memories turn into painful, emotional barbs. They flood over us like great waves of sorrow. Sights, sounds, and smells can trigger these intense bouts of grief and weeping, and there seems to be no way of controlling them. We seek relief from therapists, ministers, friends, and family, but nothing seems to help. Eventually, we search the Internet hoping to find resources to help in our time of duress. Soon we come across websites with people just like ourselves, who are in pain, who need support, and who will themselves offer support.

I think that is why most visitors to my website contact me. They are looking for immediate support and an emotional fix. I think most who write to me know that I do not have a magic wand to wave or mystical words to say to end their pain. They are not looking for an unrealistic quick fix. They write simply to see if I can explain why they feel so much more sorrow than they imagined was possible. Knowledge is power, and if they can understand why they are in such despair, perhaps they can find a way to control it.

To be sure, each case is different, and many secondary factors probably figure in. But over the years of interviewing many, many readers, I have identified a common denominator. People who grieve the deepest, who feel this intense and consuming sorrow, are those who do not just love their pets, but who love them as they love their own children.

Indeed, I found that for people like this, people like you and me, they are more than children—they are perpetual children. Like our own youngsters, they are completely dependent on us. We bring them into our domesticated, controlled environment where they have little control. We dictate their routines and provide for their needs. We feed them, give them shelter, rush them to the veterinarian when they are feeling ill. We coddle and pamper them when they seem to be feeling down. For all practical purposes, we treat them as we do our own human children. But here is the difference, they are perpetual, because unlike our own offspring, they do not grow up and leave the nest. They do not go to college. They do not get married. They do not enlist in the military. They remain in the home and continue to look to us for their provision and care. In fact, they depend on us for as long as they have breath. On our part, we are only too happy to meet those needs. For some, pets are the only children they will ever know. More than a few have confided that they were not able to have children, and that all the maternal / paternal instincts they had not been able to show actual children were focused on the family pet.

I often hear people say, "They are like members of the family." I submit to you that they aren't only like family members, but like very real and intricate parts of the family unit. They contribute unconditional love and devotion. They're there for us, to help sooth the effects of a hard day and to make us feel special. And to them, we truly are. They don't care about our bad habits. They don't care if we smoke or if we play loud music. They don't even care if we bathe or use deodorant. It's all the same to them; they're just happy to see us. If we come home in a bad mood from the day's work, they don't seem to mind. They climb right into our laps and snuggle up to us with unwavering trust.

It would seem that their whole world, their whole reason for being, centers upon us. And if you will forgive the irreverent use of this term, they readily and consistently minister to our needs. They are contributing family members who often are held in the same regard and esteem as children. Is it unreasonable then that their passing should cause us so much grief? We were in control of their lives, and somehow we lay the responsibility for their passing on ourselves. They looked to us for all their needs. They trusted us and we let them down.

The truth is, when it comes to longevity, we have no control. We cannot add one moment to our own life, let alone theirs. We may feed them the best food, walk and exercise them, get them the best veterinarian care, and spare no expense that they are safe, but when their time comes, it is their time. The mortality rate on this earth for man and animal is 100 percent. All living things pass away. There is a day that I will pass. There is a day that you will pass too. Those days are coming and nothing will stop them. We can contribute to and perhaps even control their quality of life, I am sure that exercise and healthy living increases our quality of life, but the quantity is already fixed, and when the quantity of their life is used up it is over. When that day comes, regardless of how it may happen (accident, health, etc.), it comes. As we have applied so many other human axioms to animals, so too must we apply this one as well. It is true in our lives and it is true in theirs as well.

Consequently, we should not blame ourselves. You would do well to accept and remember this. What is beyond our control is out of our control, and we are powerless to change it. That may sound redundant, but there is a significant, albeit subtle, difference. We are not in control. Therefore, we are not responsible. There is enough pain with the passing of your best friend without adding unwarranted guilt to it.

You may regret having done some things (or not done them), as I did giving Samantha that rough bath, but regret should not grow into guilt. I regret having done that in a moment of frustration, but when I measure those few moments against the years of love and pampering, it hardly matters. And this thought leads me to the last pearl of wisdom that I've learned that I'd like to pass on to you. This is one of the most ironic things between the pet and human relationship that I've learned. During their life one can see how much our pets love us, but it usually takes their passing for us to realize how much we love them. If you want to avoid the dreaded and often unwarranted pangs of guilt, don't let that be the case for you. Don't expose your heart to such regret.

Unchecked regret will lead to guilt. Regret sucks the happiness from your life, but guilt will suck the very will for living from you. Both can be avoided with very little effort on your part. Through personal experience and vicariously through the experiences of others, I have learned that most people who love their pets realize too late how important their pets were to them. It usually takes the loss of something to recognize the importance it had to us. Pets are no different. In fact, they represent the most precious losses some of us will suffer.

Accordingly, I would encourage you to be proactive in your relationship with your pet now, while your best friend is still with you. Take steps now to ensure that the sweet memories remain sweet and do not haunt you with regrets for not having displayed and demonstrated your love more when you had the time. If you do not, then I can assure you that in all likelihood you will find yourself with head in hands and tears flowing, regretting that you did not find more time to spend with the one you are so sorely missing.

Chapter 16

FINAL THOUGHTS AND ENCOURAGEMENT

Thank you for staying with me through this lengthy discourse. I realize that my superior writing skills were not what kept your attention, but rather your passionate pursuit of answers to the haunting questions that come with the loss of a beloved pet. I hope I have addressed all your concerns because I know all too well your pain, having been there many times myself. Moreover, I know that the only thing that triumphs over that pain is hope. And hope is exactly the point of this book.

Losing a precious best friend can be one of the most traumatic experiences you can have in life. I think it is clear to you by now that God views the physical death of any of his earthly creatures, animal or human, as a precious and solemn moment, and he stands in the wings ready to help and comfort any and all who will trust in him. I wholeheartedly recommend that you seek him out. He alone has peace that passes understanding. Also, other resources of comfort and support are available. There are other pet lovers who understand your pain and appreciate what you are going through. They are not able to provide the comfort and peace that God gives, but they are here and now, flesh-and-blood support resources who understand firsthand the pain you are enduring.

Sometimes it helps to be able to relate to others who can relate to you. Sometimes their stories, sad as they may be, can be a source of unexpected encouragement. You can find fellow pet people in local or online support groups. But meeting in person and sharing each other's burden is probably the best way but failing that, special chat rooms and forums online can lead to emotional and mental relief as you build relationships on the common ground of pet love, loss, and bereavement. While those words might suggest a negative common denominator, I have never heard from anyone that his or her experience with a support group was anything but positive. Moreover, many great things can come from such alliances, from knowledge about little known risks to pets to the rescue of another animal in need.

Unfortunately, there are also people, often people close to you, who do not share your love and compassion for animals and who do not understand why you are going through such anguish over the passing of a pet. Oddly, of all the articles and guides I have written to help people who love their animals, the majority of thank-you notes I have received stem from the advice I have offered regarding how to deal with friends and family who do not understand someone grieving the passing of a pet. I suppose it has something to do with the added misery that comes from a lack of compassion from those you love.

I have been a victim of a lack of sympathy and understanding when facing one of my darkest moments. In fact, as you know from my mention of it earlier, my first and best-selling book,

Cold Noses, came about as a result of the cold and calloused chiding from someone I considered a close friend, regarding the passing of a very, very dear pet. Often friends and family will not sympathize with you the way you feel they ought to. Frequently, they will react to your pain in what seems to be a most calloused way, saying things like "Get over it, it was just an animal" or "Why don't you go buy another cat?"

May I suggest from experience that you do not allow yourself to be overly upset by such responses to your pain? It usually is not meant to be personal. Human nature is rather self-centered. Everyone understands what it is to grieve, and at one time or another, we all do. It is also human nature for us to expect that those who love us will assimilate our pain and grieve with us. But that is not always true. In fact, it is not usually true.

People are quick to expect others to grieve with them, but slow to grieve with others. Everyone wants to be consoled and comforted. Knowing that someone else cares and is sharing your burden is always helpful and welcome. Unfortunately, too many of us are slow to reciprocate, if we do so at all. Somehow, the depth of sorrow we feel for ourselves is hard to appreciate in someone else. Some people find understanding your pain difficult when they are not feeling it as you do.

Again, this is human nature and it just is what it is. Most people who act this way do not mean to hurt you or make you feel worse than you already do. It is just the way people are, not intentionally, but instinctively. Then, there are other people who actually can relate to what you are going through and who genuinely try to understand what you are going through. They grieve with or for you, but who do not know how to show it. Sometimes they can come across as cold, but they do not mean to be. The onus is upon you to differentiate between those who do not care from those who do because, honestly, sometimes it is difficult to tell.

Therefore, be careful how you perceive and evaluate your friends when you are grieving. Too many people buy into that old pseudoaxiom that when the chips are down you will discover who your real friends are. While this may be true when your house is destroyed by a flood, you lose your job, or go through a divorce, I do not think it has any merit when it comes to grieving over the death of an animal.

When you are going through a divorce or hard times, people make a conscious decision as to whether they want to stand with you. When you lose a pet, often people feel your pain very, very deeply, but they just do not know how to react to your profound sense of grief. They do not know how to handle what you are going through, and they do not live up to your support expectations because they are afraid of saying or doing the wrong thing. Their first response usually is to try to cheer you up, not realizing that this is the last thing you need. When they see your negative reaction to their failed attempt, they feel inadequate and unable to help. Perhaps they even feel a little guilty for not being prepared enough to be strong for you. Or it might also just be that they feel ashamed that they came across as flippant when they really did not mean to. Just because they do not know what to do makes them no less your friend. This does not diminish their love and concern for your emotional health. They just do not know what to do.

It might take a herculean effort on your part, but you need to reach way down inside of yourself and find compassion for the friends and loved ones who seem to have failed you in your hour of need, especially if their inept attempts to help have caused you more pain. I have found that simply explaining things to them helps immensely. You might try saying something like "I know what I am going through is difficult for you too. I know you would help me if you could, but you really can't at this time. If you would just give me some time and be patient, my pain will be manageable and we can talk."

Then you need to follow through on your promise to them. Grieve as long as you must but start to focus on the positive things you have learned. Remember that your best friend is not suffering and is not gone forever. Remember that he or she is in a much better place and that this is a promise of God and not just wishful thinking. And if you are somehow holding yourself in contempt, remember that you are not responsible for their passing, so quit blaming yourself.

Turn your guilt into a hopeful expectation of reunion one day. Convert your concern for your pets' welfare to happiness over their new life. Boil your grief down to the fact that their absence is all you have to deal with and that even that will be remedied in time. In short, focus in such a way that your situation becomes more tolerable with each passing day.

May God bless your family, human and animal.

Acclaim for Alice Munro's

Too Much Happiness

"Richly detailed and dense with psychological observation.... Munro exhibit[s] a remarkable gift for transforming the seemingly artless into art.... [She] concentrate[s] upon provincial, even backcountry lives, in tales of domestic tragicomedy that seem to open up, as if by magic, into wider, deeper, vaster dimensions."   —Joyce Carol Oates, *The New York Review of Books*

"A perfect 10.... With this collection of surprising short stories, Munro once again displays the fertility of her imagination and her craftsmanship as a writer."   —*USA Today*

"Masterly.... [A] remarkable new book."
     —*Los Angeles Times*

"Daring and unpredictable.... Reading Munro is an intensely personal experience. Her focus is so clear and her style so precise.... Each [story is] dramatically and subtly different."
     —*The Miami Herald*

"A brand-new collection of short stories from Alice Munro—winner of a Man Booker Prize—is always cause for celebration, and *Too Much Happiness* doesn't disappoint. It dazzles. The ten spare, lovely tales are ... brimming with emotion and memorable characters.... Munro's are stories that linger long after you turn the last page."
     —*Entertainment Weekly* (Grade: A)

"Finely, even ingeniously, crafted.... Deliver[ed] with instinctive acuity."   —*The Seattle Times*